The Essential Equation:
A Handbook for School Improvement

David Townsend
Pamela Adams

DETSELIG

The Essential Equation: A Handbook for School Improvement
© David Townsend & Pamela Adams 2009

Library and Archives Canada Cataloguing in Publication

Townsend, David, 1942-
   The essential equation : a handbook for school improvement / David
Townsend & Pamela Adams.

Includes bibliographical references.
ISBN 978-1-55059-371-6

   1. School improvement programs--Canada. 2. Educational change--Canada.
I. Adams, Pamela, 1959- II. Title.

LB2822.8.T69 2009   371.2'070971   C2009-901560-9

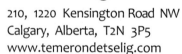

Detselig Enterprises Ltd.

210, 1220 Kensington Road NW
Calgary, Alberta, T2N 3P5
www.temerondetselig.com
Phone: (403) 283 0900   Fax: (403) 283 6947

We acknowledge the support of the Government of Canada through the Book Publishing Industry Development Program (BPIDP) for our publishing program.

We also acknowledge the support of the Alberta Foundation for the Arts for our publishing program.

COMMITTED TO THE DEVELOPMENT OF CULTURE AND THE ARTS

SAN 113-0234
ISBN 978-1-55059-371-6
Cover Design by David Casey

Contents

Chapter 4: The Essential People – Educational Leaders   61

Chapter 5: The Essential Process – Professional Development   83

Figures

Tables

Chapter 1
The Essential Equation

Introduction

In school improvement, nothing can be taken for granted, and nothing is ever as easy as its most enthusiastic proponents contend! Good ideas are usually only as good as the context into which they are introduced. Teacher-proof strategies usually end up being as friendless as their title implies. The next greatest innovation from anywhere in the world can quickly become the latest shipwreck on the beachhead of public education. All the simple solutions seem to have been tried; yet the really tough problems remain. It is a truism of school improvement that its success depends primarily on the skill and commitment of those educators who take up the challenge on a daily basis, and sustainable improvement is rarely spectacular in the short term.

We wrote this textbook in response to a demand from teachers for more specific information on how to *do* school improvement. We have attempted to distill over twenty-five years of experiences in more than 300 schools into six chapters that capture both the pragmatic and the theoretical in ways that can empower educators to take action, preferably through collaboration.

Each chapter presents one of the six essential components that, we contend, form the *essential equation* for school improvement. Each chapter offers some explanatory text, followed by a variety of materials – questionnaires, checklists, templates, and team building activities – developed or adapted through our work in schools. Each chapter concludes with a relevant case study to which is attached a set of sample questions to guide an exploration of the case.

Overview

Chapter 2 takes up the study of learning communities as the essential *structure* for enabling schools to achieve their improvement goals. The learning communities questionnaire, and its accompanying *rubric* of dimensions and characteristics of schools as communities, has been used extensively as a tool for diagnosing schools' levels of awareness, readiness, and functioning. Most educators in most schools either believe their schools are already operating as learning communities, or wish they were. The concept of the learning community is a powerful one but, when it is implemented by executive fiat, or when schools, in attempting to become learning communities, organize themselves in ways that are in sharp contradiction to the fundamental principles of the concept itself, trouble ensues. One of the reasons why some schools are unable, or unwilling, to adopt the learning communities model may be that there is too often a mismatch between the implementation process and the culture of the school. Nevertheless, we argue that when schools are moving forward in their journey to becoming genuine *learning* communities they are, at the same time, honoring a sincere commitment to be the best that they can be.

Chapter 3 makes the case that school improvement and collaborative inquiry go hand-in-hand. With its emphasis on evidence-based practice and teamwork, collaborative inquiry is the essential *method* for ensuring that the work of school teams is purposeful, focused, sustainable, and successful. Chapter 3 provides ideas and direction for ensuring that teachers-as-researchers do not get overwhelmed by the demands of data collection, data analysis, and reporting of results. At the same time, it promotes a rigorous and disciplined approach for school teams to use as they take increasing responsibility for what they are accomplishing. It champions the notion that school improvement *does not* have to be characterized as some form of add-on to the work of teachers and principals – it *is* the work, and it can be done to a level of competence that enhances the status of the whole profession.

Collaborative inquiry provides a framework for action and learning of which ongoing professional development is both an integral element and a measurable outcome. When teams of teachers organize key parts of their professional work to conform to the collaborative inquiry method, they are making a statement of hope, belief, and commitment that they will make a positive difference in student learning, and they will have the evidence to prove it.

Chapter 4 adopts the stance that educational leaders who hold formal and informal authority must take on additional responsibility for the success of school improvement initiatives. We cannot stress enough the importance of recognizing teachers as leaders in school improvement. Most of the educational leadership research applies as well to the work of teacher-leaders as it does to principals and superintendents. Obviously, teachers do not have the status that accompanies formal, positional authority and, to some extent, they do not have the same level of organizational responsibility that is attached to more formal positions. Nevertheless, for its contributions to the success of school teams and in the promotion of professional learning, teacher leadership is an essential component of school improvement.

Much of the chapter is developed around the principles of emotional intelligence and primal leadership, as articulated by Daniel Goleman. Many of the key points in this chapter grew out of the results of a series of surveys administered to superintendents, principals, and teachers over a period of nine years. An underlying premise of this chapter is that team leaders, school principals, and district superintendents have to be able to employ a broad array of skills if they are going to help move their schools forward. It does little good simply to tell people what to do. (If telling alone were truly effective, most of us would have been out of a job long ago). Leaders must show, through example, the more effective ways that the important work of schools and districts can be done. They must show they have the ability to challenge and inspire most of the people with whom they work. They have to be exemplary in matters of trust, ethical behavior, and moral purpose. In addition, they must be able to respond appropriately when anyone in their organization behaves in ways that threaten the safety and wellbeing of other employees, or jeopardize a school or district's ability to achieve agreed-upon goals. Accordingly, one of the most reliable measures of leadership effectiveness can be an ability to deal with conflict in ways that increase rather than diminish the potential for organizational growth.

Chapter 5 confronts readers with compelling links between professional development and principles of adult learning. It aligns the work of three prominent adult education theorists – Malcolm Knowles, Stephen Brookfield, and Jack Mezirow – with some of the more progressive forms of professional development. This chapter outlines how effective professional development can be embedded in the essential structure of the learning community, the essential method of collaborative inquiry, the essential focus of classroom practice, and the essential commitment to generative evaluation.

The chapter places considerable emphasis on reflection as an integral part of professional growth. For the purposes of this text, reflection is the process of studying events and outcomes to determine how they happened, why they happened, what could have been done to prevent or increase their occurrence, and what kind of impact they had. It is through this kind of reflection that educators can experience valuable insights (the great "AHA!" moments), make important intellectual connections between practice and theory, and make decisions about their teaching that lead directly to changes in practice. A central contention of this chapter is that reflection fosters the kind of learning that strengthens a commitment to action.

The Values Inventory has been included in Chapter 5 as an example of a group activity that promotes reflection while helping to build team cohesion. Teams of educators who know more about their colleagues' personal values are much more likely to find ways of collaborating that are sensitive to differences, that are based on mutual respect, and that foster the growth of trust. The careful sharing of personal information, even in matters as individually unique as values, can engender stronger feelings of empathy among educators who have already agreed to work together to complete mportant tasks.

Chapter 6 gets to the heart of this form of school improvement. The fundamental rationale for any professional development must be the enhancement of classroom practice to increase student learning. A focus on teaching and an exploration of teachers' levels of willingness or reluctance to engage in a dialogue about their own practice is what led to the creation of the alternative model of stages of concern that appears in this chapter. In the early days of our work in school improvement, we did not know just how important a clear understanding of *context* was to project success. For example, in schools where teachers are most concerned about student behavior, it is much more difficult – but not impossible – to move forward in areas of assessment of student learning, or classroom practice. Unresolved concerns increase the likelihood of interpersonal conflict. The concerns of team members must be addressed if collaborative inquiry projects are to succeed. In practice, issues of professional concern can be resolved *while* teams of teachers are engaged in the achievement of project goals, but they cannot be ignored. With its emphasis on reflection, the collaborative inquiry method fosters a bias for problem solving based on the importance of every participant's contribution to the ultimate result. If individual issues are preventing any participant from active involvement, they have to be acknowledged and dealt with in team meetings, through necessary forms of mediation, through collegial support, and through responsive leadership. The effective mediation of conflict can enhance team cohesion. It is *unresolved* conflict that threatens a team's ability to achieve its aims.

Teachers' differences of opinion about assessment of student learning have the potential to disrupt the forward momentum of virtually any school-based team. The Spelling Test has been included as a team activity in Chapter 6 because it never fails to bring to the surface most of the taken-for-granted assumptions and fiercely-held beliefs about assessment that are rarely discussed openly in schools. Once team members have experienced the Spelling Test, certainty about assessment is invariably replaced by a more productive awareness of its many dimensions and its most appropriate applications.

Chapter 7 seeks to demonstrate how the work of a school district can be shaped to gain the most benefit from all the essential elements of school improvement when they are mobilized under one overarching structure that we have identified as the essential *commitment*. The process promoted in Chapter 7 grew directly out of four years of work in one school district. We have called the process *generative evaluation* and it is, in effect, a form of school improvement that harnesses principles of adult learning, distributed leadership, professional development, the learning community, and collaborative inquiry to gather and share conclusive evidence of progress and achievement on any number of a school or district's most important goals.

Generative evaluation can employ team members from within and from outside the district, typically taking place over an extended period of time. It allows a school or district to experience the costs and benefits of doing work that is important but not perceived as being urgent. The name is truly descriptive of what the process accomplishes. Among other positive effects, generative evaluation promotes capacity building and organizational learning because it emphasizes shared responsibility over accountability, evidence over assumption, action over passivity, and commitment over lip-service. In the final analysis, it produces greater certainty among stakeholder groups that a school or district is doing what it says it is doing, accomplishing what it claims to be accomplishing.

The generative evaluation process described in the Chapter 7 Case Study covered fifteen months and gathered evidence from parts of three consecutive school years. It was conducted in a district that has been widely recognized for innovation in leadership development, induction of new staff, excellence in professional development, and consistency of improvement in student achievement. So, what came first? Was it just a fluke, a fortunate confluence of several critical components coming together all at once that allowed this district to move forward so quickly? Alternately, did district and school leaders get lucky in their choices of the "right" the models of school improvement that suited their particular circumstances, and allowed them to experience the surge of efficacy that comes with positive outcomes? In the text we note that not *all* the reasons for success in school improvement are known; that similar strategies employed in different contexts can produce widely disparate outcomes depending on a great number of variables. We argue that *programs* do not account for clear progress in school improvement nearly so much as *people* do. In this school district they had the essential match between program and people. It produced a synergy, resulting in improvements in teacher growth and student learning that stand as a testament to the ability of men and women of goodwill, when working together in enabling conditions, to make their best contribution to the achievement of the fundamental goals of public education.

Chapter 2
The Essential Structure
The Learning Community

Introduction

> The vision is, first, that the school will be a community, a place full of
> adults and youngsters who care about, look after, and root for one another,
> and who work together for the good of the whole, in times of need as well
> as celebration. The condition for membership in the community is that
> one learn, continue to learn, and support the learning of others.
>
> Roland Barth, 2001, *Learning by Heart*

The impact of the learning community phenomenon on all parts of the education system has been profound. What started as a faint metaphor passed quickly
through stages of fad and trend to become, worldwide, one of the most commonly
accepted descriptors of effective educational organizations. Moreover, it is now generally acknowledged as an essential structure under which collaborative learning
and professional growth can thrive, leading to improved student learning.

Historical Development of The Essential Structure

Perhaps only fully implemented in a handful of schools or jurisdictions in the
past few years, the concept of a learning community dates back at least to the turn
of the century and perhaps further. Lenning and Ebbers (1999) suggest that "note-
worthy proponents of learning through community have existed for centuries:

Quintilian in the first century, Lancaster and Bell in the 16th century, Comenius and The Common School Movement in the 17th century, Parker in the 19th century, and Dewey in the early 20th century" (p. 1). Our current understandings of the term *learning community* may have their origins as early as 1910 in the writings of John Dewey who contended that

> if we took instances of co-operative activities in which all members of a group take part, as for example, in well-ordered family life in which there is mutual confidence, the point would be even clearer. In all such cases, it is not the will or desire on any one person which establishes order but the moving spirit of the whole group. The control is social, but individuals are parts of a community, not outside of it. (p. 54)

The term learning community also has some connection to Schön's (1973) description of *learning systems* as institutions capable of bringing about their own transformation, and is closely related to Senge's (1990) concept of the *learning organization*. Noddings (1985) writes of classrooms and schools as *caring communities*, while Barth (1990) may be the first of many authors to use the phrase *community of learners* in purposeful reference to schools engaged in activities that support progress and innovation. Similarly, Sergiovanni (1994) contends the development of *communities of practice* may be the most effective way to improve schools. His references to communities of practice have a parallel in the theories of Etienne Wenger, who has written extensively on the characteristics of communities of practice, with particular attention to their usefulness in the change process. In the text (Wenger, McDermott, & Snyder, 2002), Wenger observes that

> communities of practice, like neighborhoods, are places where people live, think, and converse in the presence of others. It is ironic that, as we move further away from the traditional neighborhood experience in our own lives, [community is] becoming a more important part of organizational life. Perhaps some of the appeal of communities of practice is that they are an avenue through which we can recover some of our lost sense of community. (p. 74)

According to Wenger and his colleagues (2002), "it would be wrong to assume that the hallmark of an ideal community of practice would be homogeneity" (p. 35). He notes that "the kind of personal investment that makes for a vibrant community is not something that can be invented or forced. . . . the success of a community will depend on the energy the community itself generates, not on an external mandate" (p. 36). Hord (2004), one of the first to describe in detail a model of professional learning communities, lists the attributes of effective learning communities as follows:

1) The collegial and facilitative participation of the principal who shares leadership – and, thus, power and authority – through inviting staff input in decision-making

2) A shared vision that is developed from an unswerving commitment on the part of staff to students' learning, and that is consistently articulated and referenced for the staff's work

3) Collective learning among staff and application of new knowledge to solutions that address students' needs.

Richard DuFour and his colleagues have done a great deal to popularize the term *professional learning community* and to encourage its use in schools and districts. In their text *Professional Learning Communities at Work* (1998), DuFour and Robert Eaker promote a model in which schools functioning as professional learning communities demonstrate qualities that differentiate them from more traditional schools. For example, they are guided by shared mission, vision, values, and goals. Collaborative teams form their basic structure, and those teams are organized to engage in collective inquiry. With a bias for action and experimentation, members of these school communities "value engagement and experience as the most effective strategies for deep learning" (p. 4). They are committed to continuous inquiry and they assess their success on the basis of results rather than intentions. Moreover, these authors believe

> the PLC model is designed to touch the heart. Psychologists tell us that we share certain fundamental needs – the need to feel successful in our work, the need to feel a sense of belonging, and the need to live a life of significance by making a difference. The PLC speaks to each of these needs. (p. 6)

Several other authors have subscribed to variations of DuFour's model. Among them, Hopkins (2001) writes about authentic school improvement through learning communities as an approach with a relentless focus on student learning and achievement. Wald and Castleberry (2000) propose that the creation of professional learning communities in schools can be aided by the formation of collaborative learning teams "that are self-organized around topics of study that are meaningful to the individual and the vision of the school" (p. 44). In addition, they caution that "transforming schools into professional learning communities demands quality leadership – leadership that is a commitment of mind, body and spirit; leadership that is about the future; and leadership where intention becomes reality" (p. 28). Sullivan and Glanz (2006) offer a host of ideas for leading teachers' work together so that their schools might more closely resemble an effective learning community.

At the level of public policy, the learning communities model has received some uncritical support. For example, the National Commission on Teaching (2003) in the United States proclaimed that "Communities of learning . . . must become the building blocks that establish a new foundation for American schools" (p. 13). In Canada, Recommendation #13 of the Alberta Learning Commission Report (2003) "require(s) every school to operate as a professional learning community dedicated to continuous improvement in students' achievement" (p. 65).

Variables in the Essential Structure: One Size Fits All?

It is a grand assumption indeed that policy proclamation can translate a metaphor into an operating system, the mere adoption of which will render schools more effective. On one level, of course, that assumption is not open to challenge. How could a school that follows its mission and vision statements, pursues its agreed-upon goals in a purposeful way – with due regard for the values of its staff, students, and community – not be more effective than other schools that are not doing those things? If, in addition, the same school promotes closer relations with parents and community, accords highest priority to the learning of all students, and relies on data to determine its progress towards goal-achievement, how could it not be an effective and successful learning community?

Where are these schools? After visiting over 100 self-proclaimed learning community schools over a period of five years, we concluded it was rare for any one school to meet all the criteria of an effective learning community. In several, frequent collaboration occurs. In others, leadership is strong and broadly shared and, in many, commitment to evidence-based practice has been exemplary. However, most of these schools unevenly exhibit the characteristics of learning communities. It is true that most of them have mission and vision statements. All are required by law to produce education plans that incorporate school goals. Their school districts require all teachers to prepare and follow a professional growth plan that must be shared with an administrator. Many of these schools attempt to reflect and honor the values of the communities they serve, even if they are less clear about incorporating the values of staff members into operating practices consistent with the learning communities philosophy. And, while all claim to be learning communities, they vary widely in their ability to provide appropriate learning opportunities for all students, involve parents actively in the work of the school, and come to terms with the competing value-systems of government, district administrators, staff, students, and parents. In practice, the learning communities model may be based on an ideal that is unattainable for many schools, even if a majority of teachers in those schools actually have a positive disposition towards it.

Yet, the level of rhetoric and expectation – that schools will operate as effective learning communities – is so great that some school leaders feel compelled to indulge in a form of wishful thinking that has them reporting, sometimes quite fancifully, on the extent to which they see their schools operating as functional learning communities. Unfortunately, when the gap grows too wide between what leaders hope is happening and what's really happening in a school, it can trigger in staff members a negatively reinforcing downward spiral of lost opportunity, lowered morale, and increased cynicism . . . a pattern of response to change that occurs all too frequently in public education.

Many schools have recorded their determination to become a learning community through their three-year plans and annual goals, giving substance to their belief that the learning community is some form of destination. Many school staffs talk about "using the learning communities approach" to bring about change. Small groups of teachers in large-staff settings may be heard to explain how they have become a learning community even as the rest of the staff has not. School district leaders may refer to their schools as collections of smaller learning communities within a larger learning community. All of these characterizations are evidence of considerable confusion about what effective learning communities look like, and what they can accomplish. What follows is an explanation of the characteristics and dimensions of learning communities as they are found in typical North American schools.

Characteristics of the Essential Structure

Thousands of teachers attend, year after year, workshops and conferences designed to refine their understanding of and commitment to learning community philosophy and practice. Yet, before schools embark on any journey of change, all participants must recognized that profound change cannot be imposed; it must be internally nurtured to unleash the forces of innovation and the passion of individuals (Sparks, 2001). It is also important that any reconstruction process be guided by a capacity-building view of learning as opposed to a deficit model; from a perspective of creating as opposed to fixing (Mitchell & Sackney, 2000; Sparks, 2001).

An understanding of the learning community concept described in this chapter begins with a model that illustrates the interrelatedness of five important dimensions: mission and vision, leadership, learning, culture, and organizational structure (see Figure 1).

Figure 1: Dimensions of a Learning Community

Each of these dimensions has six essential characteristics as described in the following tables.

Table 1: Dimension – Mission and Vision

Characteristic	Key Question or Indicator	✓
Development	What is the process by which statements of mission and vision are created in your school?	
Commitment	Is the content and purpose of mission and vision statements reflected clearly in the goals of the school?	
Connection to Goals	Do students, parents, and all staff feel ownership of the content and intent of your mission and vision statements?	
Connection to Principles	Do the mission and vision statements honor the guiding principles of the school?	
Connection to Action	What are some activities in your school that demonstrate the purpose and goals of your mission and vision statements?	
Reflection of Values	Do your mission and vision statements capture the shared values of individuals and groups in your school?	

Table 2: Dimension – Leadership

Characteristic	Key Question or Indicator	✓
Opportunities	How many people in your school are actively engaged with leadership responsibilities?	
Availability	Through what means and with what frequency do leaders make contact with staff and community members?	
Modeling	What is the level of commitment of your school leaders to your and their professional growth?	
Risk Taking	How would you describe the willingness of your leaders to take risks to achieve organizational goals?	
Responsibility	Do your school leaders demonstrate commitment to appropriate standards of ethical and professional conduct?	
Relationships	Do your school leaders engage in and promote relationships that facilitate the achievement of organizational goals?	

Table 3: Dimension – Learning

Characteristic	Key Question or Indicator	✓
Primary Focus	Is the majority of work done in your school based on and dedicated to learning?	
Student Outcomes	What level of importance is accorded student learning and student achievement?	
Staff Outcomes	Is the expectation of staff learning linked to school goals, mission, and vision?	
Organizational Learning	How well does the school translate professional learning into enhanced effectiveness?	
Opportunities for Growth	What is the quality of connections between explicit expectations for learning and structures that support professional growth?	
Recognition	How do staff members show appreciation for each other? Does this affirm the work and worth of all members?	

Table 4: Dimension – Culture

Characteristic	Key Question or Indicator	✓
Trust	How well do staff members depend on and share responsibility with and for each other?	
Conflict Management	Are differences among members mediated in ways that enhance the achievement of goals?	
Collaboration	In what ways are staff members supported in working with each other?	
Teamwork	To what extent are the goals of the school achieved by members working with each other?	
Sense of Belonging	What value do staff members place on membership in the school community, school identity, and loyalty?	
Celebration	How do staff members show appreciation for each other? Does this affirm the work of all?	

Table 5: Dimension – Organizational Structure

Characteristic	Key Question or Indicator	✓
Communication	How effective is communication among staff members and with other schools?	
Policy	In what ways does policy guide practice and practice, in turn, inform policy?	
Planning	Are planning activities purposeful and useful in helping the school achieve its goals?	
Decision Making	Are decision makers accessible? Is the decision-making process transparent and respected by staff members?	
How Work Gets Done	To what extent do staff members accept responsibility for contributing to the achievement of organizational goals?	
Evaluation	How is the work and worth of all staff members assessed and valued?	

Assessing Your Essential Structure

As noted earlier, it is a rare school that hasn't declared itself a learning community, even in spite of evidence to the contrary. This miscalibration may be explained in several ways. On the surface, it may seem reasonable to expect that school communities can create, promote, and sustain a collaborative and collegial work life based on an appreciation for learning. However, the focused effort and constant attention required to achieve such a goal has led many schools to abandon the ideal and accommodate the pragmatic. They have come to think about the idea of a learning community less as a guiding structure and more as a terminal destination to be checked off an accountability to-do list. Such relativization of the term does not acknowledge the complex processes and levels of responsibility that must accompany efforts to create and sustain those healthy elements of community that contribute most to success.

All learning communities, like all families, are *not* functional. Importantly, the fact of their existence does not necessarily imply effectiveness. Vibrant learning communities, like healthy families, can be clearly defined and identified by specific incremental rather than dichotomous criteria. Similarly, dysfunctional learning communities are characterized by particular tendencies toward such things as goal setting, decision making, problem solving, and organizational hierarchy that are not absolute but that, more likely, fall along a continuum of effectiveness depending on a host of contextual factors.

Too often, authors write extensively about the fundamental importance of learning communities to school and system effectiveness without acknowledging the reality that there are *more* and *less* effective learning communities. Readers are too often left with the impression that once the learning community designation is bestowed on an organization, that organization now possesses all the virtues that can be attached to the title.

Identifying the Variables in Your Learning Community

Based on the characteristics described in the previous textboxes, the following survey can help members of school learning communities assess their strengths, weaknesses, and areas of effectiveness.

Figure 2: Survey – Learning Communities

Section I: Mission & Vision

Please read each statement and circle the appropriate number on the scale that best represents your experiences regarding the mission and vision of your organization.

	Never					Always
A. Mission and vision statements are developed collaboratively.	1	2	3	4	5	6
B. All members of the organization know about and are committed to the mission and vision.	1	2	3	4	5	6
C. There are strong connections between goals and the mission/vision.	1	2	3	4	5	6
D. There are strong connections between organizational principles and the mission/vision.	1	2	3	4	5	6
E. Mission and vision statements accurately reflect the values of all stakeholders.	1	2	3	4	5	6
F. There are strong connections between the mission/vision and everyday practice.	1	2	3	4	5	6

Subtotal   /36

Figure 2: Survey – Learning Communities, cont.

Section II: Leadership

Please read each statement and circle the appropriate number on the scale that best represents your experiences regarding the mission and vision of your organization.

	Never					Always
A. Opportunities for leadership are available throughout the organization.	1	2	3	4	5	6
B. Leaders are approachable and accessible.	1	2	3	4	5	6
C. Leaders model the importance of learning.	1	2	3	4	5	6
D. Thoughtful risk taking is encouraged.	1	2	3	4	5	6
E. Leaders act responsibly.	1	2	3	4	5	6
F. Leaders value and nurture professional relationships.	1	2	3	4	5	6

Subtotal   /36

Section III: Learning

Please read each statement and circle the appropriate number on the scale that best represents your experiences regarding the mission and vision of your organization.

	Never					Always
A. Learning is the primary focus of the organization.	1	2	3	4	5	6
B. Student learning is assessed using a variety of strategies.	1	2	3	4	5	6
C. Staff learning is continuous and integrated with growth plans.	1	2	3	4	5	6
D. Learning of stakeholders contributes to organizational improvement.	1	2	3	4	5	6
E. Opportunities for learning are job-embedded.	1	2	3	4	5	6
F. Learning is recognized and celebrated.	1	2	3	4	5	6

Subtotal   /36

Figure 2: Survey – Learning Communities, cont.

Section IV: Culture

Please read each statement and circle the appropriate number on the scale that best represents your experiences regarding the mission and vision of your organization.

	Never					Always
A. A climate of trust exists within the organization.	1	2	3	4	5	6
B. Conflict within the organization is managed appropriately.	1	2	3	4	5	6
C. Opportunities exist for collaboration.	1	2	3	4	5	6
D. Teamwork is encouraged.	1	2	3	4	5	6
E. Members of the organization feel a sense of belonging.	1	2	3	4	5	6
F. Celebration and recognition are integral parts of the culture.	1	2	3	4	5	6

Subtotal   /36

Section V: Organizational Structure

Please read each statement and circle the appropriate number on the scale that best represents your experiences regarding the mission and vision of your organization.

	Never					Always
A. Methods of communication within the organization support learning.	1	2	3	4	5	6
B. Policies facilitate responsible action.	1	2	3	4	5	6
C. Planning processes encourage collaboration.	1	2	3	4	5	6
D. Decision-making structures promote empowerment.	1	2	3	4	5	6
E. The work of all is goal focused.	1	2	3	4	5	6
F. Organizational improvement is evaluated in a variety of ways.	1	2	3	4	5	6

Subtotal   /36

Figure 3: Scoring Systems – Learning Communities

Scoring System 1: Dimensions of Learning Communities

Example: Please review the following example of dimensional scores and their applicable ranking. The subtotal score column contains a fictitious respondent's scores from each of the five dimensions in Part B. There is a maximum of 36 points for each dimension.

Dimension	Subtotal Score (maximum 36 points)	Ranking
Mission/Vision	29	2
Leadership	12	5
Learning	32	1
Culture	18	3
Organizational Structure	15	4

Ranking Your Results: Based upon this example, please complete your dimensional scoring by tabulating your responses from each of the five sections in Part B. Once you have inputted the scores, please complete the ranking category by assigning a 5 to your dimension with the highest score through a 1 to your dimension with the lowest score.

Dimension	Subtotal Score (maximum 36 points)	Ranking
Mission/Vision		
Leadership		
Learning		
Culture		
Organizational Structure		

Graphing Your Results: Please complete the table below using either a bar graph or a line graph format to create a visual representation of the ranking of your dimensional scores.

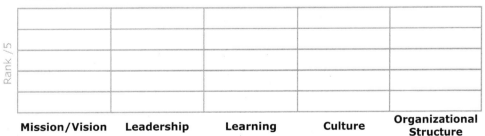

Figure 3: Scoring Systems – Learning Communities, cont.

Scoring System 2: Types of Learning Communities

Total: Please add up your total score for all of the five dimensions in Part B. The maximum total is 180.

My total dimensional score is: _____ / 180

Interpreting Your Total Score: Please check the appropriate box above the category that includes your total dimensional score. Based upon your results, you are now able to determine the descriptor that can be used to explain your current perception of the type of learning community your organization represents.

☐	☐	☐	☐	☐
1-36	37-70	71-105	106-140	141-180
Withdrawn	**Reactionary**	**Benign**	**Adaptive**	**Generative**

Diagnosing Your Learning Community

Based on the total score derived from the survey, schools may be classified into one of five different types of communities. *Withdrawn Communities* are those least likely to consistently demonstrate the characteristics of effective organizations. *Reactionary Communities* will most often exhibit unresolved conflict, frustrated idealism, and a confrontational stance toward improvement initiatives. *Benign Communities* are most often compliant and content with the status quo. *Adaptive Communities* are infused with a sense of initiative-taking, productivity and optimism. *Generative Communities* are those that consistently undertake actions that demonstrate enthusiastic commitment, mutual respect, and appreciation of inquiry.

The following rubrics give a more detailed description of each of the characteristics of the five dimensions of community. They are arranged according to type to allow you to analyze your scores on the previous two scoring calculations.

Table 6: Mission/Vision Rubric

Mission/ Vision	Withdrawn 6–12	Reactionary 13-18	Benign 19-24	Adaptive 25-30	Generative 31-36
Development	Non-participative, possibly non-existent.	Top down. In-groups and out-groups.	Statements may exist, but are rarely referred to.	Broad-based participation and recognition of statements' importance.	Inclusive, dynamic documents to which frequent reference is made.
Commitment	Few people know, few people care.	Often contrary; Often triggers argument and ill will.	Low levels of engagement and interest.	Trying to honor the spirit of mission and vision statements.	Actively living out the spirit of the mission and vision. Constantly seeking refinement and improvement.
Connection to Goals	Goals are not identified and not aligned with mission and vision.	Source of conflict. Active, generalized disagreement with the relationship between goals and mission.	Little effort expended in making these connections.	Purposeful effort at alignment. Commitment to goals is explicit.	Fully engaged in goal achievement. Connections to goals are the foundation of action.
Connection to Principles	Principles are rarely mentioned. Members may not know about organizational principles.	Another source of conflict. Principles are often situational and relativized.	Members rarely engage in discussions about these connections.	Regular reference to guiding principles. Willingness to engage in productive debate over competing principles.	Principles guide action and are constantly reviewed to test the appropriateness of connections to mission and vision.
Connection to Action	Action is idiosyncratic and rarely discussed.	Reasons for action may be highly personal or they may serve competing political agenda.	Passive acceptance of reasons for action.	Actions are undertaken with reference to principles, goals, mission, and vision.	Action is purposeful, often collaborative, and frequently promotes reflection about goals, principles, mission, and vision.

Table 7: Leadership Rubric

Leadership	Withdrawn 6-12	Reactionary 13-18	Benign 19-24	Adaptive 25-30	Generative 31-36
Opportunities	Succession planning not acknowledged. Few formalized opportunities for leadership development.	Limited. The source of disputes. Cliques prevail.	Leaders make few requests of members. Members generally do not volunteer.	Leadership opportunities are distributed. Member commitment is high.	Leadership selection is based on mission, principles, and goals as well as merit and ability.
Availability	Formal leaders are inaccessible, not frequently sought out by members.	Formal leaders avoid certain members. Gatekeeper function of leaders is apparent.	Formal positions, status and lines of communication are most obvious.	Formal leaders are accessible and visible; leaders can be contacted through informal and formal channels.	Actively engaged in the work of the organization. Decisions about availability and visibility are made purposefully.
Modeling Learning	Learning is seen as terminal and episodic, and not often relevant to all members.	Leaders' rhetoric about learning is greater than actual engagement. Efforts to model learning meet resistance.	No expectation that leaders should model learning.	Leaders are expected to be good teachers, to demonstrate their commitment to continuous learning.	Leaders are expected to be excellent teachers and lifelong learners.
Risk Taking	Risk taking and creativity are not acknowledged as valuable.	Risk-taking is minimal and discouraged by other members.	Risk taking is limited, not welcomed or recognized by members.	Risk taking is encouraged and acknowledged by all members.	Key elements of organizational learning are characterized by innovation and risk taking.
Responsibility	Behaviors are not transparent and are not seen as contributing to organizational efficacy.	Leaders frequently take credit and assign blame. Members question leaders' motives.	Leaders emphasize accountability.	Leaders are expected to set an example. Ethical expectations are high.	Leaders model standards of ethical and professional conduct consistent with organizational mission/vision.
Relationships	Professional relationships are limited, cursory, and rarely connected to organizational goals.	Relationships are used for power and control, are situational, and characterized by a lack of trust.	Relationships are formal and predictable.	Formal and informal relationships are encouraged. Mutual respect is promoted.	Leaders excel in interpersonal relations. Mentorships flourish.

Table 8: Learning Rubric

Learning	Withdrawn 6-12	Reactionary 13-18	Benign 19-24	Adaptive 25-30	Generative 31-36
Primary Focus	Greater emphasis on survival. Learning rarely discussed.	Greater emphasis on working conditions. Patterns of dispute repeat often.	Passive adherence to an emphasis on learning.	Commitment to learning is obvious.	Emphasis on learning permeates the organization.
Student Outcomes	Students appear to succeed despite the system. Students are allowed to fail.	Division between "your" students and "my" students are obvious. Results used for political reasons.	Emphasis on passing and accumulation of credits.	Students are encouraged and parents are involved. Teachers are ambitious and optimistic about student learning.	All children will learn. Learning is the primary focus.
Staff Outcomes	Rarely considered.	Great variety. Highly idiosyncratic.	Episodic attention to professional learning with low levels of staff interest.	Commitment to professional growth is high. Frequently linked to other outcomes.	Linked purposefully to goals and vision. Often collaborative.
Organizational Learning	Little interest in or understanding of this kind of learning.	Organizational memory often used for counterproductive purposes. Interpretations are opportunistic.	Not emphasized. Often shared by memorandum. Rarely discussed.	Openly debated. Used to inform future action. Shared with all stakeholders.	Source of motivation and pride. Broad sharing of results. Full involvement of members.
Opportunities for Growth	Not seen as important. External to the work of members.	Scattered, not focused. Individualistic.	Members may respond to annual lists of conferences. Limited initiative.	Coherence between goals, year plans, and professional development. Teams are common.	Fully job embedded and focused on goals. Many opportunities for collaboration.
Recognition & Celebration	Some members don't know each other. Opportunities and events are very limited.	Some want more; some want less. Some student or community events are used for political purposes. Staff events unevenly attended.	Not frequent, rarely spontaneous. Ritualized and routinized.	Frequent and meaningful. Enjoyed by participants.	Fully integrated into the work of the organization and the lives of the members. Often spontaneous.

Table 9: Culture Rubric

Culture	Withdrawn 6–12	Reactionary 13–18	Benign 19-24	Adaptive 25-30	Generative 31-36
Trust	Low levels of interaction, risk, and trust.	Episodic periods of intense inter-action. Highly personal debate. Very low levels of trust.	Moderate levels of trust. Low levels of risk-taking.	High levels of interaction, risk-taking, and trust.	Very high levels of inter-action, risk, and trust. Mutual respect is evident.
Conflict Management	Very low levels of engage-ment. "It's not my problem!"	Frequent engagement, open hostility, threats, sub-version. "I'll get even!"	Low levels of engagement. "Let's not talk about it." "Don't rock the boat."	Moderate to high levels of engagements. "*We* have a problem. Let's try to solve it!"	High levels of engagement. Resolution of conflict builds organizational strength. "Never lose sight of the goal!"
Collaborative Opportunities	Rare and not welcome.	Short term alliances for political reasons, rarely focused on learning or organizational goals.	Infrequent. Small groups may occasion-ally participate.	Frequent. Actively pursued. Often extended over long periods.	Very frequent, almost contin-uous. Engagement of all members is encouraged and rewarded.
Teamwork	Isolated events. Infrequent.	Often occurs for the wrong reasons, pitting one group against another.	Infrequent. Members do not seek opportunities.	Many different teams. Membership is fluid. Climate is supportive.	Short- and long-term teams. Highly collaborative and inclusive of all stake-holder groups.
Sense of Belonging	Many people see them-selves as out-siders. Limited sense of history.	Very low levels of loyalty. Competing claims to organizational memory. Divisive.	Low loyalty. Low levels of identification with organiza-tion.	Strong sense of identity. Agreement about collec-tive memory. Symbols are displayed.	Highly refined sense of belonging in a climate of caring. Extensive use of symbols, images, and metaphors.
Recognition and Celebration	Very low levels of interest or participation.	Individualistic. Recognition of some is often seen as the rejection of many. Dismissive.	Limited. In a good year only half of mem-bers will attend the Christmas party.	Strong empha-sis on awards, rewards, and symbols of success. Highly public displays.	Fully inte-grated into the work lives of members. Frequent and varied.

Table 10: Organizational Structure

Organizational Structure	Withdrawn 6-12	Reactionary 13-18	Benign 19-24	Adaptive 25-30	Generative 31-36
Communication Structures	Limited. Communications often ignored, or not delivered or received.	Selective, often secretive. Frequent misunderstanding and misrepresentation.	Formal, adequate, reactive.	Broad dissemination, often two-way. High expectations of involvement	Integral to organizational success. Highly interactive.
Policy	In some cases, policy does not exist. In others, it has not been reviewed for years.	Policy handbook is continually expanding. Changes to policy are frequent and very time-consuming.	Policy documents are referred to occasionally.	Policy is seen to complement goals. Members are aware of policy and often initiate changes.	Direct and constant interplay between policy and practice that focuses on people first.
Planning	Minimal, haphazard, and rarely connected to mission, goals, or principles.	Often determined by default. Very uneven, reactionary, and not always purposeful. Fosters negativity.	Sufficient to meet minimal conditions of accountability	High levels of engagement. Productive debate. Goal focused.	Very high levels of contribution by members, linked directly to mission, goals, and principles. Energizing.
Decision Making	Silence. Low levels of participation. Low levels of commitment.	Time for skirmishes, dragging up the past. Disputatious, acrimonious. Very uneven compliance.	Directive. Show of hands after little debate.	Informed debate, strong positions, and respectful resolutions. High commitment.	Continuous rather than episodic process. Highly integrated with communication structures. Valued.
How work gets done	In isolation. Minimally. Sometimes incompetently.	Grudgingly, often on members' own terms. Separately.	Without enthusiasm, individually, but competently.	Willingly and responsibly, often with others. High levels of competence.	With enthusiasm, inspirationally, collaboratively whenever possible. Synergy results.
Evaluation	Often minimal for all members. Idiosyncratic. Often counterproductive.	Highly judgmental and destructive of trust and respect. Often avoided.	Traditional and fairly formal. Moderate levels of member engagement.	Used purposefully and comprehensively. Adds value.	Constantly evolving. Fully integrated with practice. Very high levels of member engagement.

Case Study of the Essential Structure: Mr. Francis Gets the Job

The staff at Concordia School believed in the axiom "We're okay, you're okay." On the whole, they were a hardy crew of veterans confident in their ability to control and enlighten 650 adolescents, socialize a smattering of neophyte teachers, and neutralize just about any administrator. As head of the Math Department, Mrs. Hammer was fond of crowing, in reference to school principals, "We've seen 'em come, and we'll see 'em go."

When he was appointed Principal of this large junior high school, John Francis replaced a colleague who had held the position for the previous six years. A kind and gentle person, the departing principal was moving into retirement. In his first address to the staff, John's message was naively simple: "I am a different kind of principal and I hope you agree that this can be a different kind of school." Staff members were divided over whether or not to believe him. Most of them were not risk takers. Collectively, they were comfortable with their principal telling them what to do and then staying out of their way. They had predictable, time-honored mission and vision statements that they believed represented the will of most members of the community, and they were reluctant to change.

However, almost in spite of their reservations, the staff agreed to participate in some team-building and professional development activities that helped them to coalesce around a new mission, a new vision statement, a slogan, and a new set of goals for the year. After only two meetings directed by John Francis, quick agreement was reached about these important statements. Then, in a few short months filled with challenges and conversations, a subtle shift began to occur. It was given impetus when the administrative team re-arranged the school timetable to accommodate daily grade-level meetings that focused on what (almost) everyone had agreed were the school's two top priorities: student learning and professional growth. Based on the authority he felt he had derived from the evolving staff consensus, John Francis began to ask his whole staff to reconsider many of their assumptions about teaching and learning. For example, in response to a staff member's call for a change in dealing with indigenous students, Mr. Francis asked "How does that fit with our new mission and vision?" When a group of teachers raised concerns about student behavior, they were asked, "What can *you* contribute to help solve this problem?" And, when a grade level team argued for a new structure for their team meetings, they were first asked, "Can you make this part of your Professional Growth Plan?" and then, "How does this help provide a better learning experience for your students"?

Because they had become used to a previous culture characterized by complaining and blaming, many staff members were surprised by these new conversations: a few were offended, and others were unsure how to respond. Nevertheless, through making immediate and regular contact with all staff, through listening to their concerns, and through encouraging them to identify ways they thought they could contribute to the school, John Francis moved steadily forward, and the staff followed.

Each month during the first year, staff members reconfirmed their commitment to mission, vision, and goal statements. Monthly professional development meetings began with John Francis asking such questions as, "Do we still believe in the spirit and intent of these statements?" "Are these still our goals?" "Do we need to change any of these statements?" Perhaps the biggest change in the first year was a shift to shared language and expectations surrounding student learning and effective teaching. A commitment to trying to do things differently emerged. Student behavior definitely improved. Incrementally, staff members and students adapted to more effective ways of working together. At the end of the year, a majority of staff members indicated their growing appreciation for John Francis' style of leadership.

The second year could be characterized as the year of the team. Staff members increasingly embraced an ethos of collaboration and responsibility as they realized the principal would ensure that they could align their individual professional interests with the achievement of school goals. For example, sports academies were championed by staff members and, much more quickly than most teachers had thought possible, two academies – one for girls and one for boys – sprang into being. Building on the efforts of staff teams, the Fine Arts program expanded dramatically! In two grades, the academic program was refined to more effectively accommodate the unique needs of learners. The sharing of instructional materials and assessment instruments across grade levels became more pronounced. Student leadership flourished. Parent involvement escalated. The expansion of indigenous student programming provided broader services for students whom regular classroom teachers may otherwise not have had the time or skill to help. Each small success seemed to promote another successful initiative. Each team's achievements encouraged the formation of more teams.

Still, there were some staff members who changed very little, and some who resisted collaboration. They carried their wait-and-see attitude through the first two years, not openly challenging John Francis but clearly not going along willingly with the majority of staff members.

Nevertheless, the school community became more inclusive. Month by month, members of the support staff came to realize that they were seriously part of this developing community. Their voices were heard increasingly in every meeting and they became active participants in all professional development opportunities. Representatives of community agencies were seen to be much more involved in the work of the school. Word spread steadily throughout the city that Concordia school was a good place for students, and applications for registration increased accordingly.

During the third year, a broader sharing of strategies, concerns, opinions, and ideas became the way much of the work was done in C.J.H.S. While the more entrenched teachers were taking the longest to adapt, all of them appeared to change aspects of their professional behavior during this year. For example, one previously resistive teacher stepped forward and made a presentation to colleagues on preparing students for achievement testing. Two others opened their classrooms to student teachers for the first time in many years. Several invested time and effort in a re-examination of the curriculum. Others took more active interest in community events. All staff moved more willingly toward making decisions about "our students" rather than "my students." A highlight of the year was a massive and wildly successful Fine Arts Festival that involved hundreds of students and almost every staff member.

In the meantime, the administrative team continued to model shared leadership. Most importantly, they rarely responded to a staff request by saying, "You can't do it." Rather, they asked enabling questions such as, "How will you do this?" "Is this the time to do it?" They created a climate in which it was increasingly okay for teachers to step forward to take reciprocal responsibility for what they thought would help the school better meet its goals.

As increasing numbers of teachers, working in teams, challenged themselves to become more familiar with curriculum and assessment, student learning was seen to steadily improve. One simple measure of this was observed in the weekly and monthly reviews of students' results shared in team meetings. In discussions leading to decision-making, the staff moved from random uses of data to more frequent references to available data: What do we know about attendance? What do we know about parent satisfaction? What do we know about student achievement? Which students require more attention and support? Most staff became comfortable with sharing data, making sense of it, making decisions, and setting goals based on all available and relevant information.

Student behavior continued to improve over three years. The students became increasingly friendly, they interacted with adults in more respectful ways, and the incidents of gross misbehavior, as defined by office visitations and referrals, declined yearly.

The administrative team complemented each other in skills and personality. As well, they supported each other publicly even as they were willing to disagree privately. The team met daily to share information, and kept the staff fully informed about matters that affected the school. Their transparency regarding the school budget was more than most staff members expected, but it proved to be a benefit to the team when they were challenged by their Superintendent to make draconian cuts to their proposed budget for the new school year. The whole staff stood in total support of their administrators, as did the members of their School Council, who organized an unprecedented delegation to the School board. In the face of such solidarity, the Board changed its decision in favor of the school.

Through extensive role modeling, high expectations, hard work, and a consistency of enthusiasm, caring, and focus, John Francis succeeded, over time, in convincing this staff that he certainly was a different kind of principal. In turn, C.J.H.S. became a different kind of school. And then, as so often happens, John Francis accepted a new position in a new district, creating the very circumstances that can bedevil successful schools.

Would his legacy be one of continuing growth and success, or would the school lapse back into its previous culture: benign, passive, and safe? Did C.J.H.S. truly become a more effective community? Most of the staff would claim it did. Did it become better able to meet the needs of its students? Again, most of the staff are certain it did. Did C.J.H.S. become an exemplary learning community? Most staff members are sure they have embarked on a journey of learning. They like what they are becoming. Some believe they have a long way to go, while others have concluded that the journey will never end.

Ironically, when this staff was given the Learning Communities Survey at the beginning of the John Francis era, they rated themselves very high. Midway through John's term, they rated themselves appreciably lower, even as staff satisfaction with their leader and their working conditions had improved considerably. At the end, many staff members were still reluctant to rate themselves too high because, even as they acknowledged how far they had come, most of them were much more aware of how far they could go in becoming the best school they could be.

Studying the Case Study: So you think you'd like to create a learning community?

- ☑ How long can you sustain your commitment to the goal?
- ☑ What are the leadership skills and attitudes most likely to encourage commitment to a learning community?

☑ What consistent procedures and habits of mind best help staff members purposefully change toward working with others?

☑ Identify some ways that learning was the central focus of this case study.

Understanding the Essential Structure: How To Do It!

Creating Mission and Vision

1. Use the development of mission and vision statements as a model for the way in which the rest of the work will be done.
2. Keep it simple. Avoid language that dates the statements. Avoid platitudes, or sweeping generalizations.
3. Use the existence of agreed-upon mission and vision statements to authorize discussions and decisions.

Focusing on Learning

1. Assertively pursue the sustained focus on student learning. Don't let meetings on any theme, with any audience, stray too far from the topic of student learning.
2. Ensure decisions are based on collected evidence carefully analyzed and broadly shared.
3. A commitment to continuous learning by all members is synonymous with *becoming* rather than *arriving*; characterize the development of a learning community as a journey rather than a destination.

Understanding Leadership

1. Gather information, listen actively, ask authentic questions, and be seen to move forward with purpose.
2. One challenge of leadership is to ensure that people in the organization do enough – that some don't do too little and others too much. One of the great conversations leaders can facilitate is an exploration of what is *enough* for each member of the team.
3. Trust is the single most important characteristic of effective leadership.

Honoring Culture

1. Recognize and use the power of role modeling. Remember that actions speak louder than words.
2. Sincerity is the most important criterion of recognition and celebration activities.

3. The essential values of the learning community are most clearly revealed by how the least powerful members of the community are treated by all others.

Establishing Organizational Structure

1. When people are clear about what has to be done to succeed, and they adopt an attitude of joint responsibility, work gets done more willingly and more work gets done.
2. Whatever it takes to promote greater collaboration is what it takes to sustain greater collaboration.
3. Open communication requires that misunderstandings and unresolved conflict be attended to as soon as possible. Alternately, mistakes help provide compelling reasons for adopting new patterns of behavior.

References

Alberta Learning Commission. (2003). *Every child learns: Every child succeeds.* Edmonton, AB: Alberta Education.

Barth, R. (1990). *Improving schools from within.* San Francisco, CA: Jossey-Bass.

Barth, R. (2001). *Learning by heart.* San Francisco, CA: Jossey-Bass.

Dewey, J. (1910). *How we think.* Boston, MA: D.C. Heath.

Dufour, R., & Eaker, R. (1998). *Professional learning communities at work.* Bloomington, IN: National Education Service.

Hopkins, D. (2001). *School improvement for real.* London: Routledge.

Hord, S. (2004). *Learning together, leading together: Changing schools through professional learning communities.* Austin, TX: Southwest Educational Development Laboratory.

Lenning, O., & Ebbers, L. (1999). *The powerful potential of learning communities: Improving education for the future.* Washington DC: Graduate School of Education and Human Development at George Washington University.

Mitchell, C., & Sackney, L. (2000). *Profound improvement: Building capacity for a learning community.* Lisse, NL: Swets & Zeitlinger.

National Commission on Teaching and America's Future. (2003). *No dream denied: A pledge to America's children.* Washington DC: Author.

Noddings, N. (1985). In search of the feminine. *Teachers' College Record, 87*(2), 195-201.

Schön, D. (1973). *Beyond the stable state: Public and private learning in a changing society.* Harmonsworth, UK: Penguin.

Senge, P. (1990). *The fifth discipline: The art and practice of a learning organization.* New York: Doubleday.

Sergiovanni, T. (1994). *Building community in schools.* San Francisco, CA: Jossey-Bass.

Sparks, D. (January, 2001). *Leadership development key to school improvement. Results.* Oxford: National Staff Development Council.

Sullivan, S., & Glanz, J. (2006). *Building effective learning communities: Strategies for leadership, learning, and collaboration.* New York: Corwin.

Wald, P. & Castleberry, M. (2000). *Educators as learners: Creating a professional learning community in your school.* Alexandria, VA: Association for Supervision and Curriculum Development.

Wenger, E., McDermott, R., & Snyder, W. (2002). *Cultivating communities of practice.* Boston, MA: Harvard Business School.

Chapter 3
The Essential Structure
Collaborative Inquiry

Introduction

> All change is a hypothesis – a process of action, enquiry and experimentation to create a cumulative and collective knowledge about what works and how it works from within.
>
> Michael Fullan, 1998, *Leadership for the 21st Century*

Many teachers have increased their exposure to alternative forms of professional development through their involvement in varying forms of collaborative inquiry. They have accepted greater responsibility for demonstrating connections between changes in teaching practice and improvements in student learning. In doing so, they have expanded their professional knowledge and skill, contributed to an exponential increase in professional reading, and helped produce an impressive array of new learning and teaching resources.

Of course, evidence shows that the rate of change in teaching practice and other aspects of school improvement is uneven, generally slow, and difficult to sustain. Evidence also shows that collaboration within the school site may be more fraught with difficulty than has previously been identified. More positive findings show that involvement in school-based collaborative inquiry promotes greater awareness and use of curriculum documents and assessment strategies. In addition, participating teachers express increased confidence in their roles as researchers in their own schools and classrooms.

Collaborative inquiry and other forms of action research are complex ventures in joint responsibility with learning at the center and the quality of relationship as one yardstick of success. In practice, they frequently succeed in providing participants with intellectual experiences that are illuminative rather than prescriptive and empowering rather than coercive. It is not easy for groups of teachers to suspend their disbelief and commit to such forms of knowledge-generation that focus so directly on individual classrooms, and depend so heavily on the evidence of student learning that results from each teacher's purposeful efforts. Nonetheless, growing numbers of teachers are spending greater amounts of their professional time engaged in forms of inquiry because the rewards – such things as increased professional skills and knowledge, enhanced sense of efficacy and improved results – more than compensate for the effort.

Historical Development of the Essential Model

While not officially credited with authoring the term *action research*, John Dewey proposes five phases of inquiry that parallel several of the most commonly used action research processes, including curiosity, intellectualization, hypothesizing, reasoning, and testing hypotheses through action. This recursive process in scientific investigation is essential to most contemporary action research models. The work of Kurt Lewin is often considered seminal in establishing the credibility of action research. Authors such as Richard Schmuck, Matthew Miles, and Ron Lippitt developed important elements of their work with thoughtful adherence to key Lewinian principles. In anthropology, William Foote Whyte was one of the first to conduct inquiry using an action research process similar to Lewin's. In health sciences, Reginald Revans pioneered a process he called *action learning* when observing instances of social action among nurses (and, later, coal miners) in the United Kingdom. In the area of emancipatory education, Paulo Freire is acknowledged as one of the first to undertake action research characterized by participant engagement in sociopolitical activities.

The centre of the action research movement shifted from North America to the United Kingdom in the late 1960s. Lawrence Stenhouse was instrumental in revitalizing its use among health care practitioners. At the same time, John Elliott and his colleagues were championing a form of educational action research in which the researcher-as-participant takes increased responsibility for individual and collective changes in teaching practice and school improvement. Subsequently, the 1980s were witness to a surge of action research activity in Australia. Robin McTaggart describes a process known as *critical action research* in *The Action Research Planner*, Wilfred Carr and Stephen Kemmis authored *Becoming Critical*, while Stephen Kemmis and Robin McTaggart's *The Action Research Planner* informed much educational inquiry. Carl Glickman is often credited with a renewed North American interest in action research in the early 1990s, although others (Kenneth Zeichner and Richard Sagor as two examples) had been constant in their promotion of the method throughout the 1980s. Glickman advocated action research as a way to examine and implement principles of democratic governance, a move that coincided with an increasing North American appetite for postmodern methodologies such as personal inquiry and biographical narrative.

Characteristics of the Essential Model: What is Collaborative Inquiry?

Collaborative inquiry is similar to collaborative action research. The collaborative inquiry process begins when a group of educators commits to exploring and answering a compelling question about a chosen element of professional practice, followed by a cycle of examination, experimentation, exploration, and public reflection. Common threads such as the value of experience, the importance of relationships, and pragmatic sustainability are woven into collaborative inquiry. All participants bring to the process a variety of experiences that are integral to success; all forms of participant knowledge are seen as being valuable for the contributions they make to learning.

Effective collaborative inquiry is most likely to occur when teams form relationships based on trust and interdependence, and when participants bring with them effective communication skills and a common language for conversations. A climate of safety and support encourages movement from congenial discussion toward authentic discourse and, while differing opinions are inevitable, gathered evidence is used to resolve differences of perception. As Huffman and Kalnin (2003) observe, "Even in the face of disagreement [teacher-researchers] claim their emphasis on data-based decisions, and arguments [can refocus] the debates onto evidence to support decisions about teaching, rather than just opinion" (p. 573). Regardless of team composition, collaborative inquiry is most effective when initiated by individuals committed "to learn their way out of workplace difficulties" (Bray, 2002, p. 84).

Since collaborative inquiry is a form of action research, the process follows a basic cyclical format (McNiff, 2002). The journey begins when teachers-as-researchers identify an area of concern relating to their practice. The next step is often a serious challenge: pinpointing an unambiguous but deeply interesting research question. Next comes a literature search, which precedes and accompanies activities such as contemplating and communicating personal experiences, choosing a research method, and making decisions about data collection. Participants form a professional habit of asking questions about teaching practice and student learning and, as the process repeats, progress is made towards one or more facets of school improvement. The following diagram shows how one group of educators characterized their engagement.

Figure 4: Collaborative Inquiry – Action Research

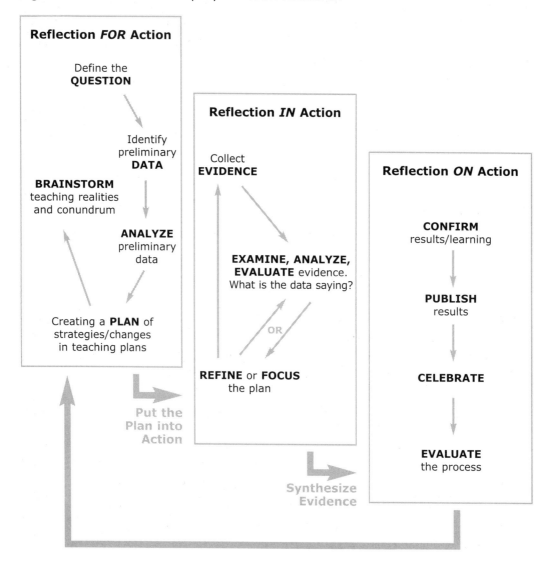

These stages are also described as learning *for* practice, learning *in* practice, and learning *from* practice. Learning for practice involves the inquiry-based activities of readiness, awareness, and training engaged in collaboratively by the researcher and participants. Learning in practice includes planning and implementing intervention strategies, and gathering and making sense of relevant evidence. Learning from practice includes culminating activities and planning future research.

Why Choose Collaborative Inquiry?

Collaborative groups in schools may include academics, teachers, and administrators; however, the inquiry focuses on questions most relevant to the teachers-as-researchers. Through their engagement in collaborative inquiry, practitioners can enjoy improved teaching practices, increased confidence, enhanced collaborative skills, and a sense of empowerment (Diaz-Maggioli, 2004; Zeichner, 2003). Additionally, collaboration among staff members can help break down the walls that often isolate educators from each other (Butler, Beckingham, Novak-Lauscher, & Jarvis-Selinger, 2004; Rogers, 2002). As teachers master the skills associated with collaboration, they begin to function more as a team – sharing, encouraging, and supporting each other. This sense of identity and belonging can profoundly impact school culture. When working together, teachers can overcome difficulties that may have previously appeared insurmountable. This sense of *teamness* increases teachers' sense of efficacy and, *together*, they accept greater responsibility for confronting challenges in positive ways.

Don't Forget the Question!

Creating a research question that is thorough, succinct, and inclusive of the diverse interests of all team members is a difficult but necessary task. The process involves often lengthy and challenging conversations that reflect the values, beliefs, and teaching philosophies of participants. These discussions are made all the more complex by the culture and history of each school. Norms and mores of acceptable professional behavior, the role of professional development, the relative value participants place on collegiality versus collaboration, and the link between professional development and student learning are all critical factors when teams are creating a research question that is relevant and unique yet still aligns with school and district goals.

Documenting Collaborative Inquiry

School-based teams need simple structures and methods to help them maintain their focus on school improvement. Events, activities, successes, and failures that do not get recorded can be quickly forgotten. As an example, a school team with which we worked several years ago chose as one of its activities a book study of a popular text. No one ever recorded that activity, participation in which was very uneven. Two years later, with many changes in membership, the school team got heavily involved in a discussion about another book study. Members were well on the way to selecting the same text when one teacher spoke up, informing everyone that they were supposed to have been there and done that two years before.

Record keeping need not be onerous. Rather, it can form an integral part of the continuous learning of the team. The following format was developed by a school district in which seven school-based teams were involved in collaborative inquiry for over three years. It shows the record of one monthly meeting of teachers, a principal, a district administrator, and a university researcher.

A Template for Sustaining the Process: Record of Decisions

This type of Record of Decisions is compiled as the meeting progresses. At the end of the meeting the recorder for the day completes a basic edit of the record, and forwards it to all participants.

Figure 5: Collaborative Inquiry – Record of Decisions

Ryter Elementary School
External Team Meeting: Record of Decisions
Tuesday, December 5

Present: Steven, David, Don, Candace, Kate, Cindy, Kathy, Pamela
Reflections: Kate reminded us of the basic question.

What have we done since the last meeting?

Task	Timeline	Responsibility
Install skylight	Complete	Don
Translate "I can" statements	Ongoing	Don
The science rubric scale is evolving	Ongoing	Don
"I can" kid statements for science unit	Ongoing with student teacher	Kate

Figure 5: Collaborative Inquiry – Record of Decisions, cont.

What have we done since the last meeting? cont.

Task	Timeline	Responsibility
Adjusted the writing scale	Complete	Cindy/Kate
Visited West Brook for Grade 5 curriculum mapping (GOs & essential questions)	Complete	Candace
Student edit & revision process	Complete	Candace
Homonym Booklet & Book of Contractions	Complete	Candace
Attend 3 Kindergarten program review committee	Complete	Cindy
Reflect on OT Kit	Complete	Cindy
ECS Conference	Complete	Cindy
Classroom visitations & planning for supervision & evaluation	Ongoing	Kathy

What have we learned?

Don: I will continue to refine the "I can" statements and will use a student to help me ensure that they are kid friendly. The presence of a student teacher has provided a new perspective.

Kate: The "I can" statements are a great basis for three-way conferences.

Cindy: The Kit is a productive way to integrate OT without pull-out. This has given a better understanding of the physiological capacities and stages of pre-school students. This helps me help with parents. It is possible to take Health Services suggestions and integrate into a regular classroom.

Kathy: We are going to each identify an area of improvement and a peer to help.

Don: I need to identify the "big," Grade 3 and Grade 4 guiding questions for writing. I need to go through the "I can" statements even more, and align them with the outcomes and post them in my room.

Candy: I need to take the students where they are and give them a little bit extra to get them ahead. Key ideas in curriculum do transcend content area information.

Kate: I learned that I over teach. Checklists are powerful and WHAT ARE MARKS, ANYWAY? With the implementation of inquiry models, what does the process approach align with – PAT's or GLA's?

Figure 5: Collaborative Inquiry – Record of Decisions, cont.

What will I do to move the project ahead?

Task	Timeline	Responsibility
Refine "I can" statements (share with students & typed)	Before Christmas	Don
Begin Math "I can" statements & Science	Immediately	Kate
Complete LA Curriculum Mapping (next 2 Workshops)	For next meeting	Candy
Move ahead on LRSD Clearinghouse	Ongoing	Stephen
Get copies of Teacher Effectiveness document	For next meeting	Stephen
Try new student self-assessments		Kate
Start "NAN does Nunavut" planning	Immediately	Kate
"Play" in my classroom!	Today	Candy
Continue to formalize supervision process; Revisit report card format	For next meeting	Kathy
Add details to OT Kit	February Meeting	Cindy
Q-Bear Book	February Meeting	Cindy
Speak to Central Office re: Cindy's kit	ASAP	Stephen

A Template for Reflection: Interim Report

As teams become more involved in collaborative inquiry, they improve in their ability and willingness to reflect – alone and together. Team members who feel they are being successful in the pursuit of their goals are increasingly more likely to see merit in taking the time to reflect, even when time is in short supply. The following form can be used to help teams gather and present the evidence of their work together.

Figure 6: Collaborative Inquiry – Reflection Guide

Reflection Guide
for
Collaborative Inquiry Projects

School: _____

Team Members

_____   _____

_____   _____

_____   _____

_____   _____

⟳ Original Question to Guide Inquiry:

_____
_____
_____

⟳ Revised Question to Guide Inquiry:

_____
_____
_____

⟳ Goal Setting

Goal 1: Improve student learning through collaborative inquiry.
Goal 2: Build capacity of team members to grow and sustain collaborative inquiry by
         providing ongoing, job-embedded professional development.
Goal 3: Implement effective teaching practices that impact student learning.

⟳ What measures are you using to provide evidence of progress toward goal achievement?

Goal 1: _____
Goal 2: _____
Goal 3: _____

⟳ What specific instruments, artifacts, or evidence has your team gathered on your journey?
(attach, if appropriate)

Goal 1: _____
Goal 2: _____
Goal 3: _____

Figure 6: Collaborative Inquiry – Reflection Guide, cont.

↻ Provide observations from your team about:

The greatest successes of the initiative thus far.
The ways these successes will be built into your project in the upcoming year.
The greatest challenges of the initiative thus far.
The lessons learned from these challenges.
The ways your team will be disseminating, over the next 12 months, information about the initiative to staff, parents, and the broader community.
The ways your team will be celebrating, over the next 12 months, what you have learned and what you have achieved.

In addition, team members can rate their progress on the Learning Communities Questionnaire (see Chapter 2) or any number of variations of that larger form, including the following example.

Figure 7: Collaborative Inquiry – Reflection for Learning

<u>Mission and Vision</u>

September 2009

6-12_____13-18_____19-24_____25-30_____31-36

February 2010

6-12_____13-18_____19-24_____25-30_____31-36

Strong Characteristics_____
_____

Characteristics Requiring Attention _____
_____

<u>Learning</u>

September 2009

6-12_____13-18_____19-24_____25-30_____31-36

February 2010

6-12_____13-18_____19-24_____25-30_____31-36

Strong Characteristics_____
_____

Characteristics Requiring Attention _____
_____

<u>Culture</u>

September 2009

6-12_____13-18_____19-24_____25-30_____31-36

February 2010

6-12_____13-18_____19-24_____25-30_____31-36

Strong Characteristics_____
_____

Characteristics Requiring Attention _____
_____

Figure 7: Collaborative Inquiry – Reflection for Learning, cont.

<u>Leadership</u>

September 2009

6-12_____13-18_____19-24_____25-30_____31-36

February 2010

6-12_____13-18_____19-24_____25-30_____31-36

Strong Characteristics_____

_____

Characteristics Requiring Attention _____

_____

<u>Organizational Structure</u>

September 2009

6-12_____13-18_____19-24_____25-30_____31-36

February 2010

6-12_____13-18_____19-24_____25-30_____31-36

Strong Characteristics_____

_____

Characteristics Requiring Attention _____

_____

Team Focus

The **Dimension** on which our team will focus: _____

The Characteristics of this dimension on which our team will focus:

_____

_____

_____

_____

Building the Cohesive Team

Collaboration is not easy, and the success of school-based teams is rarely accidental. Team members can learn more effective ways of working together by doing more work together! They can develop the discipline that collaborative inquiry demands by being more thoughtful about the interpersonal dimensions of joint work, more aware of their own needs, and more thoughtful about the needs of others. Trust is at the centre of effective collaboration and trust, like mutual respect, can be learned and earned through working together on meaningful activities that offer participants the chance to grow, to achieve, and to be more useful to others. Team-building activities should incorporate problem-solving, the need for effective communication, opportunities for shared responsibility, risk, and reward.

The following activity simulates all of these conditions. It can be completed by any number of teams of four to six people.

An Exercise in Collaboration

Each team will receive a sealed envelope containing the short story, The Paleontologist, and the five questions that must be answered. In addition, each envelope will contain all the Paleontologist's Clues. The clues should be typed on strips of paper or cardboard, one clue on each strip. As soon as every team has received its envelope, the activity starts. It is a timed event. Someone in each team should distribute the clues so that each team member has roughly the same number of clues. Then, the team task is to use the story, the questions, and the clues to solve the puzzle in the shortest time possible.

Figure 8: Collaborative Inquiry – Exercise

> ### The Paleontologist
>
> While excavating for a new highway through sedimentary rock in southeastern Alberta, a bulldozer operator unearthed what appeared to be a bone. He stopped to examine the object and showed it to his boss, who notified a friend at the local museum. Since the item looked significant, experts from the Museum of Natural History visited the site, and temporarily halted highway excavation. Museum paleontologists slowly chipped away at chalk deposits around the object and were able to release a lower jawbone with sharp-edged front teeth. The bone was straight from hinge to front and measured 74 centimeters in length.
>
> **Your team** is made up of well-known dinosaur experts, authors, and consultants who have been hired to identify the nature of the object. Using the clues provided, you must sift through the evidence to answer the following questions:

Figure 8: Collaborative Inquiry – Exercise

Questions

1. What order of dinosaur is this? **Ornithischia** or **Saurischia**
2. What type of dinosaur is it? **Triceratops, Allosaurus,** or **Tyrannosaurus Rex**
3. When did it live? **185 million, 150 million,** or **100 million years ago**
4. Was it **herbivorous** or **carnivorous**?
5. Was it **bipedal** or **quadrapedal**?

Paleontologist's Clues

ⓘ The word dinosaur comes from the Greek dinos (terrible), and saurus (lizard).

ⓘ The bipedal ancestors of all Triassic period dinosaurs gave rise to two main orders: Ornithischia and Saurischia.

ⓘ In geological terms, time is divided into sections referred to as eras. Each era is subdivided into periods, and each period is subdivided into epochs.

ⓘ Allosaurus flourished during the Jurassic period.

ⓘ In Ornithischian dinosaurs, teeth were found only on the sides of the jaw.

ⓘ Chalk is the deposit most characteristic of the Cretaceous period.

ⓘ Tyrannosarus Rex was able to bite 495kilogram chunks of meat at one time.

ⓘ Scientists learn about dinosaurs from fossils.

ⓘ Triceratops means three horned, and is one type of Ceratops dinosaur.

ⓘ Tyrannosaurus Rex was longer than its ancestor Allosaurus by approximately 2.5 meters.

ⓘ Red sandstone is typical of Triassic deposits.

ⓘ The Mesozoic Period had three time periods: Cretaceous (60 – 130 million years ago); Jurassic (130 – 170 million years ago); Triassic (170 – 200 million years ago).

ⓘ Saurischia is pronounced Suh Riss kiuh.

ⓘ Tyrannosaurus Rex was a Theropod with front legs so small they were not long enough to reach its mouth.

ⓘ Saurischian dinosaurs and Ornithischian dinosaurs differed in the structure of the pelvis. Saurischians had hips similar to those of modern lizards, while Ornithischians had bird-like hips.

ⓘ Ornithischia is pronounced Ornithiskiuh.

ⓘ Allosaurus measured 10 meters from nose to tail, and had a jaw almost 2 meters long.

ⓘ Triceratops, the last of the great horned dinosaurs, had sharp searing teeth that meshed like scissor blades to slice fibrous plants.

ⓘ Saurischian dinosaurs gave rise to two suborders of dinosaurs: Theropods and Sauropods.

ⓘ Dinosaurs appeared in the late Triassic period and disappeared at the end of the Cretaceous period.

ⓘ Theropods walked on two hind legs, and used small front legs for grasping and tearing food.

ⓘ Sauropods were herbivorous and walked on four feet.

ⓘ During the Cretaceous period, the Ceratops suborder developed from the order Ornithischia. Ceratops were herbivorous, quadrapedal, horned dinosaurs.

ⓘ Sedimentary rock is formed by layers of deposited materials that have been buried for millions of years.

ⓘ Theropods preyed on plant-eating dinosaurs, and were primarily carnivorous.

ⓘ Sauropods were gigantic dinosaurs with long necks and tails. Their delicate teeth allowed them to eat only tender plants.

ⓘ The Rocky Mountain area of Alberta was the home of many types of dinosaurs during the Mesozoic Era. At that time, it was flat with many swamps, rivers, and lakes rather than rocky and mountainous.

ⓘ Theropods had large skulls and used their large, sharp front teeth for biting food.

ⓘ Dinosaurs are a type of reptile.

ⓘ Like the modern rhinoceros, Triceratops defended itself against attack from Tyrannosaurus Rex by charging at them and using its horns as a counterattack weapon.

Case Study of the Essential Process: The Little School That Could

The future of Ryter Elementary School appeared sad but predictable. Located in a farming town with an aging population, it had moved to the top of the district's list of schools slated for possible closure. All the signs were there: few young families with school-age children were moving into the vicinity; the student population hovered around 100; teachers in the school did not live in the community; and many parents seemed to value education only to the extent that it would provide skills for their children to work in agriculture or the oil industry.

Their participation in a school-based collaborative inquiry project gave the small staff at Ryter a valuable opportunity to show how much they believed that their school had something special to offer students, and that it should stay open. Led by the enthusiasm of a young principal and a determined team of teachers, the Ryter staff demonstrated high levels of confidence with the collaborative inquiry process right from the start. They knew it might be their only chance to save the school. They planned a long-term literacy project that allowed them to focus on the writing skills of every student in Kindergarten to Grade 6. The project complemented several other initiatives that seemed to be having a positive impact on learning and student behavior in the school, and it was very well-received by most of the parents.

The Ryter Elementary team based many of their preliminary decisions on student data from a variety of sources, and they divided project-related responsibilities according to their individual expertise. As the project evolved, staff members were able to select classroom and professional development activities that were most useful and relevant to them, so they never reached a point where project-related work was seen as being "added on" to their daily duties. They looked forward to their monthly meetings with the external team members because they always had something new to share and, as they said so often, "It's great to hear what others are doing, and to hear that what we're doing is pretty good, too!"

Because reading comprehension skills were given primary focus in the research question, the kindergarten teacher struggled in the first few meetings to find a way that the project activities could be relevant to her and her young non-reading students. After three months, with the encouragement of the team and through her observations of the ways that other teachers were adapting the details of the project to fit the contexts of their classrooms, Cynthia developed a unique idea. She concentrated on the assessment of pre-literacy skills to such an extent that, before the project ended, she was able to develop a complete kit of kindergarten resources and activities that became a commercially viable product. Katherine, the Grade 2 teacher, developed anecdotal reports templates and assessment scales for reading in Grades 1 & 2. Duncan developed similar scales for assessment of literacy in science, while Christina created a detailed portfolio of assessment measures and rubrics for literacy learning in the three upper elementary grades. The project flourish quickly, and all staff members were acknowledged and honored for their innovative practices, as well as their knowledge of curriculum and assessment. Before the first year was over, they were presenting at workshops and conferences, and the materials they developed were being shared with other educators.

Parents were involved right from the start through book packs and journals, student-led conferences, and social events. They got caught up in their children's read-a-thons, and the positive impact of so much good news about student progress being regularly sent home from the school was infectious. The school's involvement in the project became a powerful talking point with parents, confirming the value of one of the project's strategies, which was to increase parental contact and awareness. As parental support for the school grew so dramatically, talk of closure became increasingly muted.

The project extended over three school years. It survived the transfer and replacement of one principal and one teacher with no loss of focus or achievement. Not only did the school stay open, sections of it were renovated in the third year of the project, as student numbers held steady in the first year, and then increased in each subsequent year, creating a need for more classroom space.

How did the staff at Ryter Elementary manage to excel in their professional learning and in the facilitation of steady improvement in student learning? First, they were provided with targeted external funding that gave the staff extra time to work together and to purchase needed resources. In addition, the Ryter Elementary principal who led the project was helpful and supportive, and very good at managing conflict. Her replacement was equally effective and committed to project success. Just as well! Although they were always professional in their work with each other, staff members at Ryter did not really get along well all the time. Sometimes they showed signs of pettiness when one or another appeared to be getting too much positive attention, or taking too much credit for project success. Sometimes they did not share information with each other as openly as they could have, causing unnecessary frustration or embarrassment for other team members. Sometimes they appeared to break into competing cliques and, occasionally, one or two team members went through short periods of disengagement. Through it all, the principals did not take sides, nor express any negative feelings in public. They were both firm and polite, inclusive in their decision-making, and generous in their affirmation of the work that was done by the whole team. Both principals found ways to be useful, ways to defuse and deflect when tensions began to rise. They acted responsibly, in an open and friendly way, and encouraged the same kind of behavior in others.

The Ryter team was also successful because they never lost their focus on student learning. The question that guided their inquiry was sufficiently inclusive to allow each team member to find a way to contribute to its answer while still honoring the learning needs of students. Improving student achievement and enhancing student learning was the most important consideration at the beginning of their project, and it was still the most important at the end. Monthly meetings always featured evidence of student work, student exam results, student feedback, or student-centered learning activities.

Furthermore, they were successful because they shared the work. Rarely did any team member come to a team meeting not having done the work he or she had agreed to do. The level of joint responsibility was high. Accordingly, they also shared the rewards, affirmation, and attention that accompanied their successes. Despite their differences, they learned that team success created more positive benefits for the school community than individual success. As the project began showing evidence of moving forward, team members became much more purposeful learners. They read more, experimented more, shared more with others, and developed levels of expertise in curriculum and assessment that made them more useful to colleagues in other schools. Moreover, they learned from their students, constantly refining their assessment and instructional practices through observation and discussion in their own classrooms.

Their commitment to project success translated into enhanced professional capacity. Here, in a fairly small rural school, a team of teachers developed skills and knowledge that lifted the performance levels of their own students and proved valuable to hundreds of other educators in many different types of schools. As well, they became competent as classroom researchers, using the evidence of their own practice to provide important new knowledge to the broader educational community.

In the end, four staff members were approached by the central office administration to transfer to other schools where they could initiate similar projects and continue to promote the collaborative inquiry process across the district. All four accepted.

Studying the Case Study: Thinking about collaborative inquiry?

☑ What contextual variables within or external to schools might impact the collaborative inquiry process?
☑ In what ways does collaborative inquiry require team members to suspend judgment about the process?
☑ How do you see this process working in your school?

Understanding the Essential Method: How To Do It!

Before the project begins:
1. Make sure all potential participants are informed and invited to be involved.
2. Make sure there is adequate funding to support all reasonable projects.
3. Involve participants external to the school: for example, district administrators, university researchers, retired educators, and parents.
4. Ensure that, as much as possible, the basic tenets of an Adaptive Learning Community are in place.

In the early days:
1. Don't let project participation be characterized as extra work. Characterize it as working differently.
2. Make sure the project responds to clearly identified needs in each school. Avoid fads. Guard against the bandwagon effect.
3. Keep meetings focused on three key questions:
   a. What have we done?
   b. What have we learned?
   c. What will we do next?
4. Protect the time and other resources set aside for project-related activities.

As the project continues:
1. Keep the learning of students and the learning of participants at the centre of project activities.
2. Make sure you have established processes for dealing with conflict, particularly through strong communication and decision-making processes.
3. Celebrate accomplishments, large and small.
4. Ensure that there is frequent reference back to the original question of inquiry.

In determining the project's impact:

1. Use all available sources of evidence, and avoid the tendency to ignore unwelcome outcomes.
2. Encourage participants to discuss and analyze their own reflections and those of their colleagues.
3. Promote the sharing of results with other educators.
4. Be seen to use project results to inform future planning.

References

Bray, J. N. (2002). Uniting teacher learning: Collaborative inquiry for professional development. *New Directions for Adult and Continuing Education, 94.*

Butler, D. B., Beckingham, B., Novak Lauscher, H., & Jarvis-Selinger, S. (2004). Collaboration and self-regulation in teachers' professional development. *Teaching and Teacher Education, 20,* 435-455.

Diaz-Maggioli, G. (2004). *Teacher-centered professional development.* Alexandria, VA: ASCD.

Fullan, M. (1998). Leadership for the 21st century: Breaking the bonds of dependency. *Education Leadership, 55*(7).

Huffman, D., & Kalnin, J. (2003). Collaborative inquiry to make data-based decisions in schools. [Electronic version]. *Teaching and Teacher Education, 19,* 569-580.

McNiff, J. (2002). *Action research for professional development: Concise advice for new action researchers.* Retrieved July 13, 2006 from www.jeanmcniff.com/booklet.html.

Rogers, A. (2002). The Nature of Learning . . . what is it? In *Teaching adults* (pp. 85-116). Berkshire, UK: McGraw-Hill.

Zeichner, K. (2003). Teacher research as professional development for P-12 educators in the USA [Electronic version]. *Education Action Research, 11*(2), 301-325.

Chapter 4
The Essential People
Educational Leaders

Introduction

> To lead is to live dangerously because when leadership counts, when you lead people through difficult change, you challenge what people hold dear – their daily habits, tools, loyalties, and ways of thinking – with nothing more to offer than perhaps a possibility.
> Heifetz & Linsky, 2002, *Leadership on the Line*

We are near the end of the first decade of the new millennium and societies around the world continue to struggle with solving their major problems. As one powerful example, despite the time and effort expended on public education, many schools remain unable to provide the quality of educational services required by large numbers of students.

Perhaps it is ironic – even inevitable – that the metaphors of leadership created in the literature so often seem to be at odds with the current context in which leaders must practice their craft. A cursory search of leadership texts yields titles with very diverse themes, such as:

Leadership IQ	Faith in Leadership
Company of Heroes	Five-Star Leadership
The Book of Leadership Wisdom	Alpha Leadership
Balancing Logic and Artistry in Schools	Shared Leadership

The Deep Blue Sea   The Journey to Authenticity and Power
Leadership Trapeze   The Contrarian's Guide to Leadership
The Leader's Journey   Leader as Learner
Nobody in Charge   Leading Without Power
Courage in Action   The Drama of Leadership
Unnatural Leadership   The Ten Commitments of Leadership
Ten New Leadership Instincts Spirit at Work
Co-Leaders: The Power of Great Partnerships

Of course, what collection of how-to guides would be complete without *Leadership for Dummies!* In many of these volumes there is growing emphasis on spirit and courage, authenticity and culture. Teams, collaboration, and sharing feature prominently, as do references to faith, hope, fables, quests, and journeys. Many of the new conceptualizations of organizational power are built around the notion of shared or distributed leadership. Alternatively, there is less emphasis on prescription, checklists, formal order and control. It is as if today's authors are telling today's leaders that they must, once again, *think otherwise* about their work, their organizations, their goals, and their roles.

Historical Development of Characteristics of the Effective Leader

A quick review of the key themes of educational leadership in the last twenty years provides some insight into the growing gap between what is hoped for and what is done in the name of leadership in schools. In the 1980s, educators socialized and trained as instructional leaders often took up their first leadership positions just in time to oversee dramatic restructuring of their schools and systems that required them to assume the primary role of business manager. While leading authors extolled the virtues of moral leadership (Sergiovanni, 1994), principle-centered leadership (Covey, 1989), and servant leadership (Greenleaf, 1979), leaders in the field were negotiating the shifting sands of societal values as they dealt with changing student populations, expanding government mandates, and burgeoning local responsibility. As Leithwood and Jantzi (1990) were writing about the potential of transformational leadership, leaders in school systems were getting familiar with the effects of massive budget cuts, new measures of accountability, progressively-disaffected staff members, and politically-empowered parents.

During the late-1990s, many educational leaders came to realize that much of the major restructuring mandated by governments had not fundamentally affected student learning. Rather, it had increased the pressures on school personnel without providing them the opportunities or the means to significantly change the learning experiences of students. Unfortunately, one of the most obvious effects of expanding government mandates was an increase in the level of hucksterism in education by those with panaceas, programs, and products to sell. Instructional leadership once again became what Blumberg (1980) had observed about supervision in the 1970s – one of public education's great non-events. Paradoxically, the more governments tried to impose system changes on public education, the less able individual principals were to perform their roles as instructional leaders. Elmore (2000) argues that

> the job of administrative leaders [is] primarily about enhancing the skills and knowledge of people in the organization, creating a common culture of expectations around those skills and knowledge, holding the various pieces of the organization together in a productive relationship with each other, and holding individuals accountable for their contributions to the collective result. (p. 15)

Yet, school principals are spending more and more time attending meetings away from their schools, and less time in classrooms and in conversations with teachers about teaching and learning (Townsend & Adams, 2007). It follows that a true indicator of the effectiveness of educational leadership should be time-on-task; specifically, the amount of time that leaders are engaged in activities with a direct link to student learning. An increased focus on system-wide approaches to educational management has dramatically reduced the amount of time that educational leaders can devote to instructional leadership. It is really an issue of balance. Recently one young principal told the story of a large elementary school in which, one Friday, all staff spent the day in an off-site workshop designed to promote greater *balance* in their lives. On Sunday, over half the teachers were back in the school, catching up on the work they had missed by attending the workshop!

Issues Faced by the Essential People

Roland Barth (2001) is an influential author whose comments about leadership resonate for formal and informal leaders alike. Barth contends that if the work of educational leaders is to create a culture hospitable to human learning, then every educator should be seeking answers to some fundamental questions such as:

- To what extent am I identifying and selecting what it is I care passionately about learning? Am I enabling others to do the same?
- Do I value and place a premium on risk taking by others? Do I provide a safety strap for those who risk?
- Who are those who model voracious, passionate learning in my school? To what extent am I such a role model?
- To what extent am I creating the conditions that allow others to construct their own knowledge? To what extent am I attempting to impart – even inflict – my knowledge on them?
- Is the education I provide for young people and grown-ups in my school inclusive of all the domains of learning, or have I selected only some portions and excluded others?
- Would I describe my school or classroom culture(s) as one(s) that foster a sense of wonder?
- Are the relationships among the students and among the adults in my school(s) collegial? Or are they isolated, competitive, adversarial?
- Do I provide for the younger and older learners assembled there a climate conducive to reflection? Are there opportunities to reflect?
- To what extent are my school cultures ones that promote authenticity? Are the "real me's" showing up among the teachers and students, or are they being checked at the door each day?
- In my school, do I attempt to maximize the variety of activities, formats, pedagogies, learning environments, and people?

Rhetorically, Barth (2001) asks,

> If the answers to these questions make explicit the conditions hospitable to human learning, why are they so dramatically unrecognized and conspicuously absent in so much of the thinking and practice in state departments of education, central offices, universities and all too many schools? (p. 164)

Richard Elmore (2000) has produced an extensive body of work detailing the effects of educational reforms on school systems and on educational leaders in North America. In addition, he has developed a model of *distributed leadership* that has been accepted relatively quickly by educational leaders in North America for its incisive analysis and pragmatic ideas. Elmore's no-nonsense tone may account for some of that appeal. For example, in commenting on the failure of policy leaders in education to understand the nature of their relationship with schools and systems, Elmore writes:

> So whatever problems of leadership might lie in the administration of schools and school systems, these problems are reflected and amplified in policy leadership. Administrative and policy leaders are joined in a codependent, largely dysfunctional relationship and, as in most relationships, the bond is strengthened by its pathology. (p. 19)

Elmore bases much of his understanding of educational leadership on many years of research and development in School District # 2 in New York City, an inner-city district in which 60% of the 23 000 students are from low-income families. His focus has been instructional improvement that, he contends, should be the primary purpose of all educational leadership. Elmore asserts that the creation of his model of *distributed leadership* would require two main tasks:

1. Describing the ground rules, which leaders of various kinds would have to follow in order to engage in large-scale improvement.
2. Describing how leaders of various kinds in various roles and positions would share responsibility in a system of large-scale improvement.

He goes on to explain that "the idea of learning to do things right" (p. 25) is at the core of a theory of *standards-based reform*, his term for many of the educational reform initiatives of the last few years. However, he says, reformers – from politicians, to policy makers, to superintendents, to principals – need to understand that the closer reforms get to individual classrooms, the less control those leaders have over the reforms' implementation and impact. The problem, for Elmore, is summed up in the following way:

> . . . how to construct relatively orderly ways for people to engage in activities that have as their consequence the learning of new ways to think about and do their jobs, and how to put these activities in the context of reward structures that stimulate them to do more of what leads to large-scale improvement and less of what reinforces the pathologies of the existing structure. (p. 36)

The Spirit of Educational Leadership: Characteristics of the Essential People

In the text *Primal Leadership*, Goleman, Boyatis & McKee (2002) expand upon concepts of leadership Goleman (1999) first developed in a book entitled *Emotional Intelligence*. He believes that effective leadership creates *resonance* in followers, while ineffective leadership creates *dissonance*. From a study with a database of 3 871 executives, Goleman and his colleagues (2002) have developed the following model of leadership containing four styles that foster resonance and two that generate dissonance.

Visionary Style moves people toward shared dreams. Its impact on climate is strongly positive and it is used most appropriately when clear direction is needed.

Coaching Style helps connect organization goals with individual aspirations. Its impact on climate is highly positive, and it helps employees improve performance by building long-term capabilities.

Affiliative Style creates harmony by connecting people to each other. Its impact on climate is positive and it helps heal rifts in a team, motivate during stressful times, or strengthen connections.

Democratic Style values people's input and gets commitment through participation. It helps build buy-in or consensus and its impact on climate is positive.

Pacesetting Style can help the organization meet challenging and exciting goals. It is used most appropriately to get high-quality results from a motivated and competent team. However, because it is too frequently poorly-executed, its impact on climate is often highly negative.

Commanding Style can soothe fears by providing clear direction in an emergency. It is most appropriately used in a crisis, to kick-start a turnaround, or to deal with problem employees. Like the Pacesetting style, because it is so often misused, its impact on climate can be highly negative.

Goleman has also developed three sets of Emotional Intelligence Leadership Competencies: Self-Awareness, Self-Management, and Social Awareness. These three clusters form the basis of the Leadership Inventory that follows. This inventory may be useful in helping school leaders assess the extent to which they are attending to many of the competencies necessary to successfully engage in collaborative inquiry for school improvement. Section III of the inventory invites readers to review their own sources and methods of professional development and rate the level of usefulness of each one.

Figure 9: Leadership Inventory

Section I: Self-Assessment

Attributes are defined as the knowledge, skills, attitudes, and behaviors that lead to effective performance. In the following inventory, three attribute "clusters" (personal, interpersonal, and leadership) are presented. For all attributes in each cluster, please rate your "Level of Present Functioning" with 1 being Inadequate and 6 being Outstanding.

<u>Cluster A: Personal Attributes</u>

Level of Functioning

PERSONAL – those attributes that relate to understanding and managing oneself.	Inadequate	Poor	Marginal	Average	Above Average	Outstanding
1. **Self-awareness:** understanding your own personality, strengths and weaknesses, and your effect on others.	1	2	3	4	5	6
2. **Emotional Awareness:** being able to speak candidly and authentically about your emotions and vision.	1	2	3	4	5	6
3. **Assessing Performance:** being aware and providing evidence of achievement of goals.	1	2	3	4	5	6
4. **Cognitive Ability:** acquiring new knowledge; recognizing subtle interrelationships; tolerating ambiguity.	1	2	3	4	5	6
5. **Decision Making:** defining and analyzing problems; knowing and using a variety of resolution strategies.	1	2	3	4	5	6
6. **Interpersonal Skills:** establishing rapport and relationships; recognizing appropriate situations for collaboration.	1	2	3	4	5	6
7. **Achievement Orientation:** working consistently towards goals and objectives.	1	2	3	4	5	6
8. **Time Management:** allocating time efficiently and effectively.	1	2	3	4	5	6
9. **Career Orientation:** achieving balance between professional and personal goals.	1	2	3	4	5	6
10. **Wellness:** meeting the demands of work without undue physical or emotional reaction or cost.	1	2	3	4	5	6

Cluster B: Interpersonal Attributes

Level of Functioning

INTERPERSONAL – those attributes that feature interaction among workers at all levels of the organization.	Inadequate	Poor	Marginal	Average	Above Average	Outstanding
11. **Team Building:** promoting and facilitating quality inter-action among team members.	1	2	3	4	5	6
12. **Motivating Others:** contributing to an environment of reward and affirmation for goal-achievement; using authority appropriately.	1	2	3	4	5	6
13. **Oral Communication:** conveying thoughts and ideas clearly when speaking one-to-one or in groups; making effective presentations.	1	2	3	4	5	6
14. **Active Listening:** attending and responding effectively to others.	1	2	3	4	5	6
15. **Written Communication:** writing clearly and effectively.	1	2	3	4	5	6
16. **Conflict Resolution:** employing appropriate conflict resolution strategies.	1	2	3	4	5	6

Cluster C: Leadership Attributes

Level of Functioning

LEADERSHIP – those attributes that relate to under-standing, managing, and leading the organization towards agreed-upon goals.	Inadequate	Poor	Marginal	Average	Above Average	Outstanding
17. **Professional Conduct:** demonstrating and promoting high levels of integrity and trust; anticipating and dealing with ethical situations and dilemmas.	1	2	3	4	5	6
18. **Visioning:** being willing to put forward a personal perspective on the future of the organization.	1	2	3	4	5	6
19. **Empowering Others:** encouraging responsibility and risk taking among stakeholders; taking a personal interest in the professional development of others.	1	2	3	4	5	6
20. **Organizational Learning:** stimulating the desire to learn and share ideas individually and in groups.	1	2	3	4	5	6
22. **Change & Innovation:** creating and supporting change initiatives that improve learning.	1	2	3	4	5	6
23. **Excellence Orientation:** developing in self and others qualities that contribute to excellence.	1	2	3	4	5	6
24. **Skill Application:** responding effectively to competing demands; attending to differences with sensitivity; translating organizational goals into workplace practice.	1	2	3	4	5	6

Section II: Perceptions of Necessary Qualities of Leadership

A list of leadership qualities is listed below. In all, four subscales (self-awareness, self-management, social awareness, and relationship management) are presented. Please rate how *important each quality is to your effectiveness* from 1 to 6 (with 1 being Not at All Important and 6 being Essential). Adapted from Goleman, Boyatzis, & McKee (2002).

Importance to Effectiveness

Self Awareness

	Not at All Important	Marginally Important	Somewhat Important	Important	Extremely Important	Essential
1. **Emotionally Alert:** ability to speak candidly and authentically about emotion and vision.	1	2	3	4	5	6
2. **Self-Evaluative:** knowledge of strengths and weaknesses; ability to welcome feedback.	1	2	3	4	5	6
3. **Appropriately Confident:** balance between self-assurance, humour, and approachability.	1	2	3	4	5	6

Self Management

	Not at All Important	Marginally Important	Somewhat Important	Important	Extremely Important	Essential
4. **Transparent:** authentic openness; integrity; confronts ethical behavior.	1	2	3	4	5	6
5. **Optimistic:** sense of proactive efficacy; views setbacks as opportunities.	1	2	3	4	5	6
6. **Adaptable:** ability to juggle multiple demands.	1	2	3	4	5	6

Social Awareness

	Not at All Important	Marginally Important	Somewhat Important	Important	Extremely Important	Essential
7. **Empathy:** listens attentively; understands multiple perspectives; appreciates diversity.	1	2	3	4	5	6
8. **Availability:** sensitive to needs of all stakeholders; behavior in a mode of service rather than authority.	1	2	3	4	5	6
9. **Contextual Astuteness:** politically and socially aware; understands unspoken agendas and values.	1	2	3	4	5	6

Relationship Management

	Not at All Important	Marginally Important	Somewhat Important	Important	Extremely Important	Essential
10. **Inspiration & Influence:** articulates a shared mission; creates excitement and collaboration; adept at positive persuasion; develops and mentors others.	1	2	3	4	5	6
11. **Change Agent:** recognizes need for change; offers solutions to barriers; maintains a large and inclusive view of the future.	1	2	3	4	5	6
12. **Conflict Management:** shows understanding of all perspectives; acknowledges views and feelings of all sides; redirects energy towards shared ideals.	1	2	3	4	5	6

Section III: Sources and Methods of Continuing Professional Development

Below is a list of sources of professional development. First, please indicate whether or not you use the source or method in your *own* professional growth by checking either "Yes" or "No" in the space provided. Then, indicate your assessment of the usefulness to you of each source or method of professional development by circling the appropriate numeral from 1 to 6 (with 1 being the least useful and 6 being the most useful.)

Level of Usefulness

	Yes	No	Not At All Useful	Marginally Useful	Occasionally Useful	Useful	Extremely Useful	Essential
1. Books by leading authors	☐	☐	1	2	3	4	5	6
2. Educational journals	☐	☐	1	2	3	4	5	6
3. Other educational publications	☐	☐	1	2	3	4	5	6
4. Collaboration with colleagues	☐	☐	1	2	3	4	5	6
5. University Courses	☐	☐	1	2	3	4	5	6
6. CD-ROM and other computer-assisted learning materials	☐	☐	1	2	3	4	5	6
7. Personal Internet access	☐	☐	1	2	3	4	5	6
8. Workshops	☐	☐	1	2	3	4	5	6
9. State or Provincial conferences	☐	☐	1	2	3	4	5	6
10. National conferences	☐	☐	1	2	3	4	5	6
11. International conferences	☐	☐	1	2	3	4	5	6
12. Engagement in action research	☐	☐	1	2	3	4	5	6
13. Individual Profession Growth Plans	☐	☐	1	2	3	4	5	6
14. Project Leadership	☐	☐	1	2	3	4	5	6

Understanding the Results: Implications for Leading Collaborative Inquiry

Leaders high in emotional self-awareness know how their feelings affect them, their job performance, and those with whom they work. They are attuned to their guiding values and they are candid and authentic in discussing them with other members of their teams. School leaders who rate high in this competence typically know their strengths and limitations. They can accept constructive criticism and feedback and they exhibit a sense of humor about themselves, as well as a relative perspective about the importance of the work. In projects that employ a collaborative inquiry model, such leaders are able to play to their strengths, and will often welcome difficult assignments. They have a self-assurance that lets them stand out in a group.

A defining characteristic of emotional intelligence can be seen in leaders who stay calm and clear-headed under high stress or during key moments of the collaborative inquiry process that involve disagreement, conflict, or emotional disengagement. Such leaders are open to others' feelings and beliefs. They build their integrity by openly admitting their own mistakes and confronting unethical behavior in others. When dealing with the ambiguities that are an inevitable part of school life and the process of collaboration, effective leaders maintain their focus and energy. They see school improvement as a means, not an end, and display an enthusiasm that extends to their persistence in learning and teaching ways to do things better. Perhaps one of the most important attributes of leaders who effectively implement collaborative inquiry school improvement is their view that many of the problems that arise can be treated as opportunities for learning rather than barriers to progress. They expect that purposeful change will make things better.

Effective leaders of collaborative inquiry can sense the unstated emotional levels in their teams. They are more likely to be able to use diversity as an asset, and they are better able to contribute positively to the growth of social networks as they honor the importance of relationships. Critical to the success of collaborative inquiry is a leader's ability to move people to follow a compelling vision or a shared mission. Effective leaders promote a sense of common purpose in ways that generate commitment across groups.

Lastly, these types of leaders view the collaborative inquiry process as an opportunity to develop the talents of others; they take time to understand others' goals, their strengths and their weaknesses, and they are often the school's educational mentors and coaches. In recognizing the need for change, they are able to challenge the status quo and champion the new order, all the while finding practical ways to overcome resistance to change.

Effective Leadership at the District Level

The success or failure of school improvement initiatives that employ a collaborative inquiry process is impacted by many factors, working alone or interacting in various combinations. Timing is an influential variable, while craft knowledge, morale, history, and trust are but a few of the other elements that play a part in stimulating or eroding participant readiness, engagement, and commitment. Of course, the individual school context is critical, but so are such factors as the expertise and commitment of school and district leaders. Too often, the role district leadership plays in helping or hindering the work of schools is overlooked. Most school superintendents clearly do not have the power to bring about positive change in individual schools but, just as clearly, they do have the power to prevent schools from following their chosen path to improvement if that course challenges the superintendent's view. Most district office administrators strive to develop relationships with schools that are based on mutual respect and usefulness but, to be consistently effective, they must walk a fine line between practices that support *bureaucratic accountability* and those that promote *joint responsibility*. In reality, more effective district-level leaders are able to apply strategies that integrate varying dimensions and facets of emotional intelligence.

The chart that follows was created during a long-term study of school improvement initiatives, many of which attempted to employ collaborative inquiry methods. It describes several other operational indicators that offer insight into the impact of district leadership on the ability and willingness of schools to participate in successful collaborative inquiry projects.

In District A, those few educators who were involved in a leadership capacity developed a strong sense of loyalty to the professional development strategy the district was following. School administrators who felt they were part of the collaborative inquiry experience were positive in their commitment and support, while many of those who had not been so involved felt marginalized. A large majority of teachers did not experienced the benefits of full participation in projects; nor did they engage in any process of inquiry that promoted collaborative action.

In District B, a great deal of time was lost early in the process when indecision was the order of the day, and teacher and principal commitment to the process was compromised. There was a wholesale change of district leadership at the end of the first year of funding. The newly-appointed central office team found it was extremely difficult to overcome considerable resistance and a general lack of trust in their schools. They made a strong public commitment to pursue a course of research,

Table 11: Operational Indicators: District Leadership and School Improvement

	DISTRICT A	DISTRICT B	DISTRICT C
Leadership style	Centralized, hierarchical	Centralized, partially distributed	Partially centralized, broadly distributed
Level of Teacher Engagement	Small groups of educators experience intensive levels of participation	Invitational. Unevenly dispersed from very high to very low	Broadly dispersed with high levels of participation and autonomy
Models of Professional Development	Broad based by theme. Marginally related to daily teaching responsibilities. Episodic.	Focused. Partially job embedded. Opportunities unevenly accessed.	Job embedded. Opportunities are extensive. PD is focused and sustained.
Organizational Structures	More vertical than horizontal.	Still quite vertical, but enabling and encouraging.	More horizontal with balance between central and site-based decision making.
Project Philosophy	Improved student learning through teacher professional growth.	Improved student learning through improved teaching practices.	Improved student learning through evidence-based practice.
Project Goals	Fragmented. Not closely aligned with school and district goals.	Linked to district goals rather than school goals.	Aligned with provincial, district, and school goals. Integrated with teacher growth plans.
Responsibility versus Accountability	Low accountability, low responsibility for most participants.	Moderate levels of accountability and responsibility for most participants	High commitment to responsibility, generalized recognition of the value of accountability.
Communication	Direct and one-way.	Invitational, but limited.	Two-way. Invitational, transparent, and responsive.
Role of Inquiry	Not necessary to project success.	Backwards by default.	Purposefully planned. Essential to the success of every project.
Collaboration	Intensive collaboration within small groups, often off-site.	Expanding collaboration in selected subject areas, across schools.	Expansive collaboration across schools, projects, and subject areas, on and off-site.

inquiry, and action that was consistent with the original intent of the funding initiative but, after three years, progress across their schools was very uneven.

Leadership in District C made effective use of resources in ways that demonstrated unequivocal support for sustained and cyclical collaborative inquiry. There was a purposeful emphasis on distributed leadership, capacity building, shared decision making, collaboration, learning, results, and professional responsibility. District leaders worked closely with their schools to show that staff involvement in collaborative inquiry contributed directly to increases in student learning and teacher growth. Relations between schools and district leaders were characterized by open communication, transparency, and rising levels of trust. A commitment to the achievement of project goals extended across the district, and the celebration of project successes became an integral part of the district culture.

While they did not extend to every school, the successes enjoyed in District C were commendable. They were spearheaded by a group of leaders who promoted the following conditions of collaborative inquiry:

- Shared vision
- Clear goals
- Appropriate measures
- Focus on learning
- Distributed leadership
- Collaborative inquiry-based practice.

The case study that follows was selected because it extends the concept of effective leadership at the district level. It shows one educational leader's depth of understanding of several of the operational indicators in Table 11, and the skills she exhibited in overcoming barriers for school improvements.

Case Study: Joan Greenshields Takes up the Challenge

What happens when an entire school district loses faith in its Central Office administration? Principals become anxious. Teachers become disaffected. School board members do not get voted back into office in the next election. Parents band together out of fear and anger. Students, especially those in high school, lose hope and trust. By the time the lawyers have agreed on buy-out conditions, the locks have been changed, and a provisional leadership team has been installed, a phenomenal amount of goodwill has been lost, and staff morale has plummeted.

Joan Greenshields found herself in just such a set of circumstances when she became the Acting Superintendent of Big Plains School Division. Joan had not sought the senior administrative position. She had taken the position mainly in response to an impassioned request from her new School Board Chair, and expected to serve only as long as it took for the new School Board to make arrangements for her permanent replacement. Joan was a former teacher, vice principal, and principal in this district, a calm woman with a friendly disposition and a reputation as a team player.

Despite her temporary status, Joan set about dealing with those matters of concern that could not be left unattended any longer. In her own words, the experience was like playing with one of those carnival pop-up games – every time she thought one issue had been solved, two or three others would jump up in random fashion and demand her attention. She quickly realized that she alone could not deal with all the challenges the district faced so, not being the kind of person to just sit and wait, she asked for and received permission from the School Board to hire more staff to help her tackle some pressing problems.

In choosing her assistants – those educational leaders who would become key players in the district – Joan surprised many of her former colleagues. She did not play it safe. Rather, she selected three educators known for their energy, enthusiasm, and integrity, all of whom were relatively young for district office leadership. Each brought particular skills and strengths to these new positions. Under Joan's guidance, they quickly came together as a team and established themselves as strong advocates for students and teachers. They planned together, worked together, and learned together. Strong bonds were formed during the first summer when they worked out a plan for their district. They began the new school year full of clear purpose and strong commitment.

While she was building capacity at the district level, Joan was equally involved with her school administrators. It wasn't so long ago that she had been one of them. She knew what they wanted from their superintendent and their district office staff, and she had some firm ideas about the nature of the working relationships she wanted to develop with the whole group and with individual principals. She was very deliberate, making school visits a centerpiece of her leadership, and taking every opportunity to talk informally with principals, vice principals, teachers, support staff and students. She wanted to know as much about them as she could. Most of them, in turn, were impressed by the sincerity of her interest.

Joan's commitment to student learning, something that had always guided her own practice, blossomed dramatically as she gained confidence in her new role. She became a powerful advocate of professional development for all staff. The district office was transformed into a centre for learning. Teams of teachers gathered there regularly – before, during and after school – to learn from and with each other the new content and methods that were to inform the work of dozens of school teams that were forming in response to the support, encouragement, and direction flowing from the district office.

Joan made monthly visits to each of the district's twenty-one communities, often in the company of School Board members and her fellow administrators. She promoted the efforts of School Councils, and formed the district's first School Council Committee made up of representatives from every School Council. Joan worked as hard to serve the School Board as she did on any other part of her job. It was a time of building trust and confidence, of trying to move forward, even though people were afraid they might make a mistake. It was a time of learning, too. There was so much Joan had to learn about district governance and management; there was so much new School Board members had to learn about school operations and public education. Joan was patient and respectful, always ready to apply the criteria of fairness and reasonableness to every difficult decision. As the political and administrative lessons were being learned, a new spirit of cooperation and mutual respect was seen to grow in the district. It was apparent in principals' meetings, at professional development workshops, in the emerging focus on student learning, and in school-community relations as well. In the midst of this, the School Board decided that Joan would be the district's permanent Superintendent.

Near the end of the first year, Joan and her team met with the School Board to confirm the district goals, the pursuit of which would guide district operations for the coming year. It was during these deliberations that a new motto took shape. The district had once been known for "leading the way in public education." With Joan as Superintendent, it became the district "where students are our present and our future." School administrators welcomed the change in language almost as much as they welcomed the changes in planning. For the first time in their collective memory, they were able to go into their summer recess with a very clear idea about the district's plan because they had been involved in the decision making through which it was formulated. They now had time before and during the summer to think about and work on their own school plans.

For Joan and her team, the summer was a time for looking back, looking forward, and recharging. In their conversations, team members spoke about the importance of balance in their lives. They were thrilled to have the opportunity to work hard in such a great workplace but they all knew the dangers of burnout; Joan, in particular, was careful to set an example that emphasized a time for work, a time for play, a time for family, a time for community, and quiet time. She was an excellent role model.

A brief review of Joan's progress should not convey the impression that everything came easily, and everything worked perfectly the first time. She faced many challenges and dealt with many situations she did not feel prepared to handle. The first time she had to help a former colleague decide it was time to retire weighed heavily on Joan. The first time she had to dismiss a district supervisor for harassment, she agonized over the decision. Some of the appeals of a student suspension, or expulsion, with which she had to deal challenged her fundamental belief that schools had to be able to serve the needs of every student. Some of her contacts with angry parents left her frustrated and hurt. Nevertheless, the successes enjoyed by staff and students in the first year of her tenure gave Joan confidence that the district was moving in the right direction, and she was helping provide the kind of leadership that suited the district's needs.

At the beginning of her second year, when it was becoming increasingly apparent that she had really grown into the position, Joan spent several days in September visiting every school and every classroom to deliver a school calendar to every student. Some superintendents from other districts were less-than-gracious when they heard what she had done, but Joan never appeared to worry unnecessarily about what others thought of her. Most of her teachers and principals were impressed with her effort, knowing as they did just how much extra time it required. She did it because she felt it was important that every student should have some form of personal contact with the school superintendent.

In her second year, Joan took up a concern that she had shared with other administrators when she was a principal. It had to do with the district's decision-making process. It seemed there was always some degree of discontent over which decisions were made at the district level and which could be made at the school level; which decisions could be made by large schools and which of the smaller schools had to defer a larger number of decisions to the district office. Joan suggested a series of meetings with only one purpose: to establish agreement on those decisions that had to be made by district leaders, those that had to be made by school leaders, and those which required a different form of adjudication. It should not have been so surprising that the School Board, the district office administrators, and school leaders were able to come to such an agreement. There was goodwill on all sides and a rising level of trust. The decisions that were reached in these meetings were to have a profoundly beneficial impact on the district before the year was over.

Late in January, an acrimonious dispute between the Teachers' Association and the government erupted into a full-scale strike. All districts were affected. Many school boards reacted by locking out their teachers in an attempt to preempt a second round of rotating strikes. For two weeks, the education system was in turmoil. Feelings of hostility and helplessness, anger and revenge intruded into the ongoing debate about the reasons for, and effects of, the various moves and counter-moves by teachers and their employers. Joan's district was caught up in the battle. Schools were locked. Some teachers walked the picket lines. Parents were outraged. It looked as if a lot of goodwill was being washed out of the system. After two hard weeks, the schools reopened, but feelings still ran high and it was obvious a lot of damage had been sustained.

As soon as the strike was over, Joan brought together representatives of the Teachers' Association, principals, parents, and School Board members to develop a contingency plan so that such a disruption would never again threaten district friendships and relationships the way this strike had. It was typical of the way Joan chose to act as superintendent. She took the most responsible course she could devise, in the shortest amount of time, so that conflicts were not allowed to go unre-solved and cause additional damage. She moved events forward as one among equals, a reasonable and caring person who clearly put students first. She did not let her message get distorted or misinterpreted. She was clear and she was fair.

Near the end of that year, Joan was once again confronted with a difficult situa-tion. At lunchtime, two high school students in a rural community had bullied and badly beaten a fellow student. The injured student was taken to hospital. The other students were arrested. News of these events spread quickly. Joan did not hesitate. She went immediately to the school, conferred with the principal, and agreed to share the responsibility for dealing with the large contingent of television and news-paper reporters who converged on the scene. On television, Joan appeared con-cerned, responsible, and in charge. Her answers were polite and direct. Her message to the community and to all of the parents was unambiguous: "We will deal with this matter in a way that will be a positive example to others."

Joan is still the superintendent. In five years, schools in her district have shown increasing success in all measures of school improvement, from parent and commu-nity approval ratings, to teacher satisfaction, to student achievement on standard-ized tests. Of greatest significance to this text is the fact that Joan's district continues to lead all others in the amount of money it spends on professional development per employee. Many members of her school and district teams have moved on to other positions in other districts. As they have been replaced, the established standards of performance have been reinforced. People who work in this district know they are expected to strive to be as good as they can be. People who work in this district rate it as "an excellent place to work."

Studying the Case Study: So you want to try educational leadership?

- ☑ How do leaders translate their beliefs about schooling into action that impacts every classroom?
- ☑ What are some of the skills needed to mediate broad differences of opinion in ways that lead to purposeful action?
- ☑ To what extend are you willing and able to give educational leadership the time and the effort it requires?
- ☑ Who are your role models for effective educational leadership? National leadership? World leadership?

Comparing and Contrasting Approaches to Essential Leadership: How To Do It

Relationships
1. Rely more heavily on face-to-face relationships than on bureaucratic routines.
2. Model desired classroom practice in administrative actions.
3. Model desired classroom practice in collegial interactions.

Accountability
1. When schools and systems attempt to bring about change, it helps to promote models of responsibility rather than accountability.
2. Engage deliberately in capacity building and promote collective learning.
3. Acknowledge differences among communities, schools, and classrooms within a common framework of improvement based on student learning.

Responsibility
1. Maintain a consistent focus on instructional practice. Create an environment in which adults take responsibility for the academic performance of children.
2. Focus first on a limited number of instructional areas and practices, becoming progressively more ambitious over time.
3. Evaluate performance on the basis of all students, not just selected groups of students.

Direct observation and analysis
1. Make direct observation of practice, analysis, and feedback a routine feature of work.
2. Ensure these activities take place in a safe environment, a climate of trust.
3. Centre group discussions on the instructional practices that are at the heart of the work of the school.

Even as this brief chapter nears an end, questions must linger about method and strategy. Simply stated, "How can the work of school improvement and change be done best?" Of course, there are no easy answers. "Through learning" is not adequate. "Through caring" is similarly not enough.

Yet there may be something that offers direction in the following paraphrase of the writings of Matt Ridley (1996), from his book *The Origins of Virtue.* Ridley suggests that if we build organizations in which people are not expected to take *joint responsibility* for the work that their organizations do, we may engender in them no obligation, duty or pride, and may impose only obedience instead. Where authority replaces *reciprocity* (Ridley's word for the *tit-for-tat* of responsible human interactions), people may be encouraged away from instincts that foster the greater good and towards those that foster self-interest and anti-social behavior. Ridley believes people are not so nasty that they need to be tamed by intrusive external agencies. He suggests that too much government, on the other hand, can bring out the worst in people. In particular, he speculates that too much external control can subvert human instincts for building social cooperation. In Ridley's analysis, the collapse of community spirit in the last few decades may be attributable to too much government. His answer lies in "devolution: devolution of power over people's lives to parishes, computer networks, clubs, teams, self-help groups and small businesses – everything small and local. . . . Let everyone rise and fall by their reputation" (p. 264). Ridley (1996) concludes his argument with the following exhortation:

> Just as trade between countries is the best recipe for friendship, so exchange between enfranchised and empowered individuals is the best recipe for cooperation. We must encourage social and material exchange between equals for that is the raw material of trust, and trust is the foundation of virtue. (p. 265)

References

Barth, R. (2001). *Learning by heart.* San Francisco, CA: Jossey-Bass.

Blumberg , A. (1980). *Supervisors and teachers: A private cold war.* Berkeley, CA: McCutchan.

Covey, S. (1989). *The seven habits of highly effective people.* New York: Simon & Schuster.

Elmore, R. (2000). *Building a new structure for school leadership.* New York: The Shanker Institute.

Goleman, D. (1998). *Emotional intelligence.* New York: Bantam.

Goleman, D., Boyatzis, R., & McKee, A. (2002). *Primal leadership.* Boston, MA: Harvard Business School.

Greenleaf, R. (1979). *Servant leadership.* New York: Paulist.

Heifetz, R., & Linsky, M. (2002). *Leadership on the line.* Boston, MA: Harvard Business School.

Leithwood, K. & Jantzi, D. (1990). Transformational leadership: How principals can help reform school cultures. *School Effectiveness and School Improvement, 1*(4), 249-280.

Ridley, M. (1996). *The origins of virtue: Human instincts and the evolution of cooperation.* New York: Viking Press

Sergiovanni, T. (1994). *Building community in schools.* San Francisco, CA: Jossey-Bass.

Townsend, D., & Adams, P. (2007). *Inquiry into school improvement: A research & development approach.* Claresholm, AB: Livingstone Range School Division.

Chapter 5
The Essential Process
Professional Development

Introduction

The best thing for being sad," replied Merlyn . . . "is to learn something. That is the only thing that never fails. You may grow old and trembling in your anatomies, you may lie awake at night listening to the disorder of your veins . . . you may see the world around you devastated by evil lunatics, or know your honour trampled in the sewers of baser minds. There is only one thing for it then – to learn. Learn why the world wags and what wags it. That is the only thing which the mind can never exhaust, never alienate, never be tortured by, never fear or distrust, and never dream of regretting. Learning is the thing for you."
T. H. White, 1987, The Once and Future King

Engagement in diverse and sustained professional development activities is essential if teachers are to understand and effectively manage the children, contexts, and challenges that are characteristic of today's schools. As increasing numbers of students and parents are forced into the realization that their world is changing in ways that will influence attitude and behavior in every corner of public education, they will come to count even more on their schools and teachers to help them find new ways of surviving and thriving in a new social system. If there ever was a time when teachers could be content with their levels of knowledge and skills, and pay scant heed to the need for continuous learning, that time has certainly passed. Teachers have joined all the other leading professions in honoring the value of timely learning that allows a profession's members to maintain their usefulness, and sustain their professional expertise over the course of a whole career. In practice, continuous educational professional development is based on an awareness that, while educators may be at many different stages in their learning, they can all participate in and benefit equally from the professional growth journey.

Professional development for educators is one of the most important factors in improving student learning. It may take many forms, including one-day workshops, ongoing study groups, university courses, research and development initiatives, peer-mediated learning, and mentorship. One effective way to promote and nurture learning and growth for all members of a school community is through the creation of a collaborative and collegial workplace in which all members are engaged in learning. The metaphor of the learning community discussed in Chapter 2 has emerged as a compelling one that encourages, supports, and directs educators who are engaged in professional development. However, regardless of the model chosen to guide professional development opportunities, there can be no denying its primary purpose: the improvement of student learning.

Historical Development of the Essential Process

In 1999, the American Council on Education (2002) emphasized the need for "strong, well crafted professional development opportunities" for practicing teachers (p. 24). Effective teaching is increasingly being viewed not only as competent practice, but also as professional reflection and inquiry, willingness to learn and grow, and an unshakable commitment to student learning. Yet, even as teachers are moving towards a collective practice of teaching (Blasé & Blasé, 1998) and narratives of their work (Clandinin & Connelly, 2000), the delivery methods used in most professional development experiences have remained unchanged for several decades.

Professional Development as Rationalism: "Sit n' Git"

Professional development activities of this nature are based on the role of the teacher as a passive receiver of information that is disseminated by a perceived expert. In this linear and transmissional mode of delivery, teachers are considered pedagogically *tabula rasa*. While it may be efficient (consider the keynote speaker tradition used in conferences and conventions), this type of professional development removes the locus of control for teachers' learning to an external source and limits the likelihood that there will be noticeable change in teaching practice.

Under this framework, teachers' experiences and perceptions of their classroom reality are valid only to the extent that they conform to a larger set of accepted truths about effective teaching. Consequently, these kinds of professional development experiences are often irrelevant to and incongruent with teachers' "real life" understanding of the dynamics, challenges, and joys of teaching.

Professional Development as Behaviorism: "Give it a Try"

Stimulus-response theories of teaching and learning guide behaviorist frameworks of professional development. The same theories are fundamental to many teacher preparation programs. Behaviorist professional development experiences assume that effective teaching can be defined by skills that can be mastered, observed, and evaluated. At their worst, they consist of short, episodic, and unsustained workshops that are highly focused on one particular technical aspect of teaching, such as writing Educational Plans for students with unique learning needs or improving student comprehension skills. At their best, they are voluntary in-service opportunities based on a series of ongoing themes identified by past participants or veteran teachers as being critical to the improvement of teaching. Typically, these programs follow a process of explaining the specific skill to be developed, demonstrating the skill, immediate feedback from an observing expert regarding the level of skill completion, and successive re-try and feedback iterations until an appropriate level of competence has been demonstrated.

Peer assistance, paired learning, and coaching are often used in behaviorist professional development. Technical feedback is one hallmark of this approach, as is segmented learning via case studies and "one correct answer" problem solving.

Professional Development as Constructivism: "Work it Out Together"

The concept of constructivist learning is usually attributed to Vygotsky (Fosnot, 1996), who asserts that knowledge of teaching is perspective-bound, and the result of multiple contextual variables. It contends that understanding is temporary, developmental, internally constructed, and – central to this textbook – socially mediated.

In this type of professional development, teachers are encouraged to raise questions about their classroom practice. Then, in conversations with colleagues and a professional development facilitator, teachers realign their understandings or, alternately, reconstruct models that accommodate several explanations of their classroom reality. Experimentation is encouraged and, because the locus of control for determining success is primarily internal, constructivist professional development appears more likely to foster lifelong learning and individual responsibility for self-learning.

Constructivist professional development is built on principles of collegial sharing and sense-making. Participants are expected to be actively involved over an extended period of time. The inclusive nature of the process assumes that teachers may choose a wide selection of topics, exploring them through such strategies as mentoring, peer mediation, group investigation, video observation, micro-teaching, or pedagogical problem solving.

This model accepts that teachers come to professional development experiences with a diversity of knowledge, feelings, and skills, sincere and genuine in their efforts to understand what they can contribute and what they can learn as they interact with peers. Over time, through activity, reflection, and educative dialogue, participants are able to examine their assumptions about the teaching and learning process. As they confront their own beliefs, and those of other educators, participants are involved in a learning process that eventually allows them to reconstruct a philosophy of teaching and forms of professional practice that resonate in greater harmony with their daily classroom experiences.

Barriers to Effective Professional Development

Apart from the constraints of time and resources, a commitment to professional development can be subverted by many other factors. Examples of these include:

- *Lack of Awareness* that can create resistance when unexamined assumptions about students, pedagogy, or self inhibit possibilities for growth.
- *Stress* that can result when educators are constantly being told what to do. Growth is more likely to occur if educators can take responsibility for choosing what to do.
- *Distrust* that thrives in a culture of judgment and criticism. Growth requires a fair amount of risk taking, which, in turn, depends on trust.
- *Fear of Failure* that can lead to inaction, subversion, and disengagement, as educators resist taking responsibility for choices and changes.
- *Competing Demands* that have to be acknowledged and addressed. An inability or an unwillingness to differentiate between work that is *immediate* and

work that is *important* will ensure that professional development takes a back seat to almost everything during the course of a school day, or week, or year.

- *Impatience and Pessimism* that can be the result of natural dips and plateaus in the improvement process have to be expected and anticipated. Leaders committed to school improvement must be able to respond appropriately to tried-and-proven strategies for derailing commitment that might include any or all of the following:

    "I *told* you this wouldn't work!"

    "We've already tried that!"

    "This is exactly what I've been doing for the last ten years!"

    "That simply won't work with my kids!"

    "It's just the latest fad!"

    "This emphasis on student achievement takes all the fun out of teaching!"

    "Leave us alone and just let us teach!"

- *A Longing for the Good Old Days* that can engender over-dependence on the past and its associated nostalgia, undermining efforts to move forward.

Of particular interest in our work is the concept of *unitas* (Edwards, 2004) in which characteristics of effective adult education, professional development, and community intersect in a process of inquiry. Many conditions, strategies, activities, and phases of professional development are associated with adult learning and with the ideals of a community of learners.[1]

Figure 10: A Newer Model: Professional Development as Adult Learning

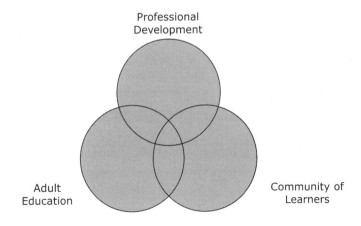

Professional
Development

Adult
Education

Community of
Learners

---

1   This term, attributed to Etienne Wegner, is different in both substance and intent from others' terms such as professional learning communities, learning organizations, or cultures of learning.

Prominent theories of adult learning and community may contribute to more meaningful professional development experiences for teachers, particularly those that relate to Knowles' *andragogy*, Brookfield's *reflective practitioner* and Mezirow's *transformative learner.*

Andragogy: The Work of Malcolm Knowles

Knowles' (1984) explanation of andragogy encompasses the views that

1) Each adult learner must be assumed to be autonomous with the capacity for self-improvement, independent of social structures and pressures.
2) Each adult learner possesses unique and individualistic experiences and needs that become antecedents to learning.
3) Each adult learner brings individual differences to the learning experience that are to be respected and nurtured to achieve intellectual fulfillment.

As Pratt (1993) summarizes:

> We are thus presented with a portrait of adult learners largely separate from their cultural and historical contexts, capable of controlling and directing their learning, and expected to develop according to their own idiosyncratic paths or potential. (p. 17)

Knowles (1984) outlines seven elements of the "andragogical process design" (p. 15) that assist educators of adult learners to facilitate a successful educative experience, involving them in (1) climate setting, (2) mutual planning, (3) diagnosing their own needs, (4) formulating their learning objectives, (5) designing learning plans, (6) carrying out their learning plans, and (7) evaluating their learning.

Knowles' theory can guide the professional development of teachers in several ways. He promotes growth experiences that are characterized by respect, trust, support, authenticity, and negotiation, and contends that "it is the responsibility of a facilitator to provide a caring, accepting, respecting, helping social atmosphere" (p. 17). Knowles is one of the first authors to provide compelling theoretical reasons to explore professional development structures that present alternatives to one-way, knowledge-disseminating rationalist models.

Critical Reflection: The Work of Stephen Brookfield

Brookfield (1984) concludes that adult learning, in the form of either formal or informal professional development, is a much broader and deeper event than either participants or facilitators have typically believed. He describes two general categories of learning: the *individual mode* in which adults engage in self-teaching, voluntary learning and, eventually, more sophisticated methods of self-directed learning; and the *group mode* that integrates several types of community and liberative experiences. Brookfield (1986) contends that through engendering "a spirit of critical reflection" (p. 10), professional development for adults should aim toward "the nurturing of self-directed, empowered adults. Such adults will see themselves as proactive, initiating individuals engaged in a continuous re-creation . . . rather than as reactive individuals buffeted by uncontrollable forces of circumstance" (p. 10). Brookfield acknowledges that, while this process creates certain amounts of cognitive and emotional dissonance, the absence of this type of teaching "denies the essentially transactional nature of teaching-learning, and pretends that challenge, creative confrontation, and (sometimes painful) self-scrutiny have no place in adult learning" (p. 146).

Transformation: The Work of Jack Mezirow

Mezirow (1990) developed the theory of *transformational learning* based on his curiosity about the construction, validation, and reformation of *meaning*, and its place in the learning experiences of adults. He contends that transformational learning theory provides a foundation for understanding adult learning and professional development as an emancipatory process that encourages learners to become aware of their awareness. He suggests,

> Its goal is to help learners move from a simple awareness of their experiencing to an awareness of the conditions of their experiencing . . . and beyond this to an awareness of the reasons why they experience as they do and to action based upon these insights. (p. 197)

The essential element in creating awareness is learning through critical reflection. As (adult) teachers engage in professional learning experiences, they begin to reflect on assumptions underlying their identity as learners.

To fulfill the goals of transformational learning, Mezirow lists several suggestions for the facilitation of adults' learning:

- Progressively decreasing the learner's dependency on the facilitator.
- Helping the learner understand how to use resources and how to engage in reciprocal learning relationships.
- Assisting the learner to define learning needs.
- Assisting the learner to assume increasing responsibility for defining learning objectives.
- Helping the learner organize what is to be learned with what is relevant.
- Emphasizing experiential, participative, and projective instructional methods. (p. 200)

The clear direction promoted by these and other authors for facilitators of teacher professional development is toward a more negotiatory and differentiated type of engagement in learning activities. Mezirow concludes that "every adult educator has a responsibility for fostering critical reflection, and helping learners plan to take action" (p. 357).

The Role of Reflection in Professional Development

Donald Schön (1983, 1987, 1988) has done much to promote the concept of teachers as *reflective practitioners*. In school improvement teams, teachers often resist the idea that their deeper thoughts about some aspect of practice are worthy of public sharing. Many teachers are uncomfortable revealing their levels of thinking about professional practice lest they be seen by their colleagues to be ill-informed or less aware. Part of the responsibility of any school improvement initiative must be the promotion of a common language of practice and discourse that enables participants to share their thinking more thoroughly and more clearly.

The Role of Values in Promoting Collaboration and Reflection

As teachers experience more of the positive aspects of reflection, they become more willing to examine their own taken-for-granted assumptions about teaching and learning, about students, and about the reasons why they have their own particular sets of values and beliefs. The following activity is one that provides teachers with a complex array of insights into their own worldview, and the personal belief systems of their colleagues. It can be done first as a self-assessment, but it has the potential to promote greater trust when it is used by colleagues working together to enhance mutual respect.

Figure 11: Activity – Inventory of Values

An Inventory of Values

Each of the groupings below contains five values descriptors. In the space beside each value, place a numeral from 1 to 5. Numeral 1 represents your lowest ranking value in that group. Numeral 5 represents your highest ranking value in that group. Each value descriptor **must** be rated with a different numeral.

1.
_____ Achievement
_____ Compassion
_____ Justice
_____ Spirituality
_____ Prosperity

6.
_____ Honesty
_____ Understanding
_____ Authority
_____ Expertise
_____ Prosperity

11.
_____ Compassion
_____ Physical Wellbeing
_____ Understanding
_____ Ethics
_____ Leisure

2.
_____ Compassion
_____ Independence
_____ Integrity
_____ Authority
_____ Status

7.
_____ Achievement
_____ Emotional Wellbeing
_____ Trust
_____ Ethics
_____ Authority

12.
_____ Ethics
_____ Status
_____ Spirituality
_____ Expertise
_____ Wisdom

3.
_____ Creativity
_____ Trust
_____ Leisure
_____ Status
_____ Prosperity

8.
_____ Charity
_____ Independence
_____ Understanding
_____ Trust
_____ Spirituality

13.
_____ Charity
_____ Compassion
_____ Creativity
_____ Emotional Wellbeing
_____ Expertise

4.
_____ Charity
_____ Justice
_____ Leisure
_____ Authority
_____ Wisdom

9.
_____ Charity
_____ Compassion
_____ Creativity
_____ Emotional Wellbeing
_____ Expertise

14.
_____ Achievement
_____ Charity
_____ Physical Wellbeing
_____ Honesty
_____ Status

5.
_____ Independence
_____ Emotional Wellbeing
_____ Prosperity
_____ Physical Wellbeing
_____ Wisdom

10.
_____ Emotional Wellbeing
_____ Justice
_____ Understanding
_____ Traditions
_____ Status

15.
_____ Achievement
_____ Indepedence
_____ Traditions
_____ Trust
_____ Expertise

<table>
<tr><td>

16.
_____ Achievement
_____ Compassion
_____ Justice
_____ Spirituality
_____ Prosperity

</td><td>

18.
_____ Physical Wellbeing
_____ Justice
_____ Trust
_____ Integrity
_____ Expertise

</td><td>

20.
_____ Achievement
_____ Creativity
_____ Understanding
_____ Integrity
_____ Wisdom

</td></tr>
<tr><td>

17.
_____ Creativity
_____ Physical Wellbeing
_____ Traditions
_____ Authority
_____ Spirituality

</td><td>

19.
_____ Emotional Wellbeing
_____ Honesty
_____ Integrity
_____ Leisure
_____ Spirituality

</td><td>

21.
_____ Independence
_____ Creativity
_____ Honesty
_____ Justice
_____ Ethics

</td></tr>
</table>

Scoring Profile

The numbers of the groupings in which each value occurs are indicated in the five scoring columns.

☐ Transfer your scores for each grouping
☐ Add the scores horizontally, and record totals for each value (no total should be higher than 25 or lower than 5).
☐ Rank your values from highest to lowest.

Value Descriptor						Total Score for this value	Ranking for this value
Achievement	1	7	14	15	20		
Authority	2	4	6	7	17		
Charity	4	8	9	14	16		
Compassion	1	2	9	11	13		
Creativity	3	9	17	20	21		
Emotional Wellbeing	5	7	9	10	19		
Ethics	7	11	12	16	21		
Expertise	6	9	12	15	18		
Honesty	6	13	14	19	21		
Independence	2	5	8	15	21		
Integrity	2	16	18	19	20		
Justice	1	4	10	18	21		
Leisure	3	4	11	13	19		
Physical Wellbeing	5	11	14	17	18		
Prosperity	1	3	5	6	16		
Spirituality	1	8	12	17	19		
Status	2	3	10	12	14		
Traditions	10	13	15	16	17		
Trust	3	7	8	15	18		
Understanding	6	8	10	11	20		
Wisdom	4	5	12	13	20		

Beyond Construction

School-based teams that are able to achieve agreed-upon goals through a commitment to evidence-based practice can be seen to engage in many of the forms of adult learning described and defined by Mezirow, Knowles, and Brookfield.

Figure 12: Professional Development as Inquiry and Action

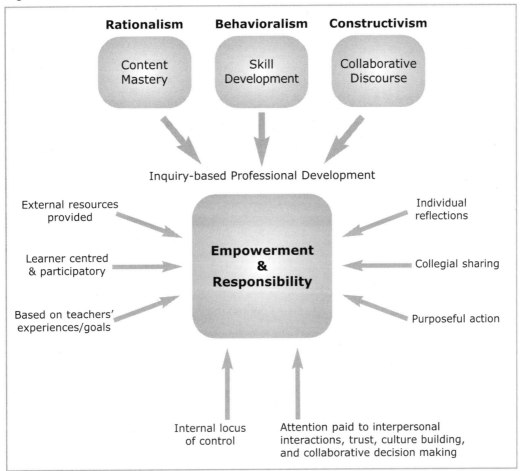

Figure 12 outlines our provisional conceptualization of the way many elements of professional development can influence participant efficacy. This model emphasizes evidence-based responsibility, rather than document-based accountability. Specifically, accountability models tend to encourage activities such as inappropriately weighted use of student achievement data, episodic and terminal professional development events, formalized record-keeping of participation in professional development activities, relatively low levels of interaction and relationship-building opportunities, and high levels of dissonance between institutional goals and individual professional aspirations. Alternately, the inquiry-based model highlights the need for professional development to be job-embedded, with sustained opportunities for individualized and differentiated activities emphasizing *learning* rather than *change*. In the inquiry-based model professional growth is recognized through individually developed professional learning plans that are aligned with school goals, principles and values.

A second element of this type of inquiry is a purposeful inculcation of various reflective habits. In addition, this inquiry model recognizes the value of collaborative opportunities for guided conversation and sense-making to encourage action. Through successive cycles of goal-setting, re-visioning, and the integration of new knowledge, teachers control their growth. This is a process that does not happen on demand, nor to prompting through a checklist approach. It involves a certain amount of personal disclosure, as questions are raised and answered, over time, to make clearer the bridges between professional development, teaching, and learning.

How does this inquiry model fit with today's schools? The following set of ten indicators of effective schools, compiled through direct observations in many school sites from 2000 to 2009 would seem to provide a most hospitable substrate for the promotion of collaborative inquiry.

- Each year begins with a thorough clarification of individual and group responsibilities, expressed in terms of goals to be achieved that are in agreement with mission and vision and in harmony with school values.
- The nature of relationships (e.g. teacher to teacher; teacher to administrator; professional staff to support staff; all staff to students; student to student) is obvious. Members of the school community know how to act and interact with each other in ways that promote mutual respect.
- For all staff, personal growth is an essential element of agreed-upon goals. Professional growth plans and professional development initiatives are directly linked to school goals.
- Critical elements of workplace culture are explicit. That is, there is generalized knowledge and agreement about "the way we do things around here," and there is a strong sense of purpose.
- Learning is a primary outcome, and the assessment of achievement and learning guides the work of the school.

- Collaboration is the means by which many important tasks are accomplished. Formal and informal professional development activities promote collaboration.
- Individual responsibility is the principle that guides school community members in their commitment to work.
- Productive management of conflict is a characteristic of interactions among group members.
- The growth of trust results from the purposeful pursuit of agreed-upon goals. In turn, it is a very important measure of school effectiveness.
- Opportunities for celebration and recognition of goal achievement and personal growth are integral to the life of the school. The assessment of goal achievement is a continuous process.

Further to the compilation above, those who aspire to lead schools in improvement initiatives might want to explore the proposition that many of the problems associated with school improvement – like many of the difficulties that arise in classrooms – are directly attributable to something that people in positions of responsibility fail to do, or do not do well enough. Leaders in school improvement act in ways that honor and affirm the work of others. At the same time, they are skilled in conflict management and resolution, meaning that they know how to deal with colleagues whose attitude and behavior threatens the school's ability to accomplish its goals. When school leaders are seen by their staff members as willing and able to deal appropriately with negative, reactionary, or disengaged staff members, they contribute to the development of trust and a heightened sense of staff efficacy. When leaders fail in this regard, they contribute directly to mistrust and demoralization. Often there is no neutral ground in these matters. Schools are either moving forward in their ability to achieve their goals, or they are stuck, in which case they are becoming less effective. Staff members will not commit fully to professional development activities in a school where emotional safety and personal trust are in jeopardy.

Similarly, leaders of school improvement initiatives are seen to be effective communicators. In practice, that means they listen well, present clearly, and respond appropriately in their interactions with other members of the school community. However, while active, attentive listening is a very powerful communication skill, listening alone will not always provide others with the kinds of assurances they want that leaders have the courage and the wisdom to act responsibly on things they have heard. In school improvement, timing is important: there are times when people in leadership positions must be the first to take action. In addition, staff members want their leaders to be forthcoming and sincere in their compliments, to avoid unnecessary advice, to eschew taking credit for the work of others, not to pass the buck, not to play favorites, not to dominate the airwaves, and not to be petty. In short, they want their leaders to be quite remarkable!

In return, staff members and leaders who share a mutual respect are much more likely to collaborate, to work responsibly toward the achievement of goals, and to champion the value of professional development. As well, they are more likely to demonstrate a high degree of institutional loyalty, for that characteristic is largely dependent on the extent to which staff members feel they are part of a community. Conversely, many of the things that upset staff members can be traced to issues of ego, self-esteem, status, and belonging that, left unchecked, can trigger patterns of behavior that inflict discomfort on others and damage group cohesion. Effective leaders of school improvement are able to read and respond to most of the signals they receive from others. In the process, they are better able to re-focus attention on those aspects of the work of the school that provide the greatest opportunities for success and celebration.

Finally, if a school staff is not ready to proceed on an professional development initiative, and the school leaders are not capable of moving the initiative forward, then the responsibility falls to district leaders and other authorities to act ethically, in the best interests of students and parents, and begin the tough work of educational leadership that will create the necessary conditions for change. Schools that cannot engage in productive, continuous professional development fail to thrive. Our bottom line has to be that there is no excuse good enough to allow schools to fail.

Case Study: High School Confidential

A few years ago at an educational conference, a young school superintendent was honored as Administrator of the Year. In his acceptance speech he paid tribute to all the principals and teachers who had helped him earn the award and concluded by saying, "Now, clearly, our next great challenge is to be just as successful with some of our *high* schools!"

Evidence of sustained improvement in high schools is sparse. When Fifteen Thousand Hours was published in 1979, there was a sense of hope among educators that the knowledge and skills necessary to bring about change in high schools were within the reach of most school districts. Thirty years later, most high schools haven't changed much at all.

The school that is the subject of this case study started out in 1985 with all the advantages. It was a brand new school in a state-of-the-art building. The administrative team had been hand-picked. Department heads and teachers had been subjected to a rigorous selection process, after which they were given several months to prepare for their grand opening. Nothing was spared in ensuring that this school would offer its 1500 students the best educational services they could get.

Yet, in less than ten years, all the hopes of excellence had vanished. The school had flourished briefly, then quickly settled into mediocrity. Principals came and went. The movement of staff in and out became so predictable that one long-serving teacher suggested their school was more like a military staging camp than an educational institution! District superintendents tried every quick-fix solution that came along. None worked.

After twenty years, the social and economic make-up of the community had changed dramatically; the school was home to students representing over 130 nationalities, there had been four principals in the last six years, and staff morale was at an all-time low. The 2005 high school final exam results provided one last big shock: out of twenty-four high schools of similar size and similar student demographics, this one ranked at the bottom. In the staff meeting organized to discuss the results, one teacher said, sarcastically, "Well, someone's gotta be last!"

Almost out of desperation, the administrative team decided to try to stimulate teacher professional development by getting involved in a school-based team project sponsored by the district office, with funding from the Department of Education. Carefully, they involved key teachers from all subject areas in preliminary discussions about ways to proceed. They were hoping to get a certain level of "buy-in" before the naysayers and the more vigorous opponents of any proposed change could exercise their considerable political power over the rest of the staff. Many of those teachers had been at the school from the very beginning. Their standard response to any hint that they should do anything differently was to trot out oft-told stories of the good old days when they were in charge of their professional lives and they were treated with respect.

The staff meeting at which all teachers had their chance to be heard on the subject of school-based teams was not a long one. Twenty-five teachers – mostly fairly young – indicated their willingness to be involved in this form of professional development. Several teachers sat at the back of the room with their arms folded and said nothing. A few made derisive jokes. A few showed some deep hostility toward administrative team members in particular. At 3:15 P.M., the majority of staff members stood up and made a fairly obvious point of leaving the meeting before the principal had finished his concluding remarks. The meeting ended with four teams of teachers and their administrators agreeing to meet again the following week, when substitute teachers would be provided and each team would have 90 minutes to start on their plans for professional development.

One team decided to concentrate on developing course units and common exams. Another wanted to try exchanges of classroom visits. One team wanted dedicated time each week when they could plan together. The fourth team wanted to implement several new ideas to influence student behavior. An administrator was assigned to each team. Timelines and activities were planned for the next month.

In a subsequent meeting, the administrative team decided to use one of the school's upcoming professional development days to try to encourage more staff members to get involved in the team project. They felt that they needed to provide opportunities for team building and the kind of structured discussions that might lead to some resolution of conflict, and some amelioration of bad feelings among staff members. The date was set, the last Friday of the month. A school team was formed to plan the big PD Day. External consultants were hired. A variety of activities – ranging from intellectually challenging, to physically invigorating, to very social – were designed to appeal in some way to every member of staff.

The day began with a hot breakfast and ended with beer and wine. In between, most staff members suspended their disbelief, shed some of their inhibitions, set aside some of their cherished rivalries, and enjoyed themselves. In their exit surveys, 65 out of 82 participants rated the event as *very good* or *excellent.*

Nevertheless, by Monday morning much of the goodwill had evaporated. One staff member had sent a strident message to all staff berating them, and the administrators in particular, for wasting public money on "totally useless, non-educational frivolities", and threatening to reveal this shocking waste to the city's taxpayers through a letter to the newspapers. A few others had their own negative comments to make in the staff room and the hallways. Predictably, many of those who contributed to the day, and felt it was valuable, were incensed by this negativity, and showed their hostility by openly confronting their colleagues. Rifts that had shown signs of healing were suddenly widened. People took sides. Gossip spread. Rumors flew. Any good that might have grown out of Friday's experiences was washed away as staff members retreated into those patterns of behavior that had become time-honored in this culture of dysfunction. People cried. People yelled. People locked themselves away in their rooms. Student punishments escalated.

The administrative team members also behaved as before. They made public accusations against those teachers they knew had always opposed them. They shuttered themselves away for long periods during the next few days so that it appeared as if no one was really in charge. They were accessible neither to those who wanted to continue arguing with them, nor those who wanted them to show some courage and face down the people who were intent on stopping change.

Within two weeks, only two teams remained intact. In two more weeks, it was decided that the school-based teams idea should be left for another time. An assistant principal went on stress leave. The principal announced he was applying for early retirement. Dozens of teachers indicated they would be applying for a transfer at the end of the year.

Studying the Case Study: Is it the process?

This case study is a good example of paradoxical intention. School leaders and committed staff members did not set out to create the chaos and dysfunction that ultimately prevailed. Their intentions were honorable, their goal clearly evident. Still, they underestimated the power of entrenched and withdrawn staff members to derail their best efforts and, in the end, fell victim to a form of demoralization that threatened their professional commitment to students and colleagues alike. What went wrong?

Proponents of the improvement concept misread the whole staff's level of readiness, failed to anticipate the strength of the forces of opposition, and did not heed the lessons that should have been learned from a short study of the school's history. Pragmatically, those people in positions of leadership did not possess the level of moral authority, or respect, that might have allowed them to move the initiative forward. The informal leaders in the school were politically stronger than the formal leaders, whose lack of leadership skills was abundantly evident even before the initiative began.

Most importantly, no one seemed to have any functional awareness of the role of professional development in the lives of many of these educators. Decisions were made based on false assumptions, misunderstandings, and vain hope, not necessary prerequisites for any kind of success. The model of professional development in this high school was disarmingly uncomplicated: teachers engaged in the amount and type of professional development they believed was right for them. After the first year or so of the school's existence, there were no whole-school initiatives, few attempts to implement a cohesive program based on collective need or desire, and no examples of cooperation among staff save for a few subject-area teams that existed for short periods of time. For many years, large sums of professional development funding had been carefully shared among all staff members, to be used as they saw fit and, in recent years, substantial additional funds had been expended with little record of how the money had been spent, or evidence of any results that its use had produced.

☑ Can you accurately assess the levels of awareness and readiness for professional development in your school?

☑ Do your formal leaders have the essential knowledge, skills, authority, and respect to lead your school in sustained professional development initiatives?

☑ Can your staff achieve consensus on those aspects of student learning and/or teaching practice that could benefit most from ongoing professional development activities?

☑ Can you identify the most successful professional development initiatives you have ever experienced? Why were they so successful?

Understanding the Essential Process: How To Do It!

One way to summarize the message of this case study is to compare what happened with what we have seen in more effective schools. The following statements apply to those schools that have demonstrated the ability to provide sustained, high quality educational programs and services to the great majority of students who come into their care.

Try to . . .

1) Be an informed participant in research, professional development, and school improvement.

2) Align your Individual Growth Plan goals with the learning goals of your students and the goals of any improvement project with which you are involved.

3) Align your professional development activities with the learning that is most relevant to your work, your growth plan, and your school goals.

4) Engage in and contribute to collaboration, even if you only work closely with one or two other staff members.

5) Be curious about the evidence of your work and its effects on learning.

6) Talk more about the things you *will* do rather than those you will not do.

7) Ask questions, keeping in mind the difference between a question for which you already think you know the answer and the other types of questions!

8) Share your learning with colleagues. If you are learning something new and exciting, there's a good chance it will be equally interesting to many other educators.

9) Be generous with colleagues as they try to improve their professional practice. A few kind words at the right time can make a big difference to the effectiveness of teams.

10) Remember, *what goes around comes around*. We're all struggling with some aspect of our professional practice. We need support, encouragement, and a climate of trust as we try to get improve and grow.

Try to avoid . . .

1) Having more goals than you can realistically handle. Many beginning teachers have dozens of goals. More experienced teachers try to concentrate on two or three goals each year.

2) Looking for the single best way to teach everything. There are often many ways to achieve high levels of effectiveness in classroom practice.

3) Adding professional development activities to an already overburdened schedule. If you add some things, you should try to drop some others.

4) Getting discouraged if some things you try don't seem to work at first. That can be a good opportunity to share your experiences with others, so that learning can be increased and your own burden lessened.

5) Losing sight of the goal. The goal is learning for everyone.

References

American Council on Education. (2002). *Touching the future: Transforming the way teachers are taught.* Washington, D.C. Author.

Blasé, J. & Blasé, J. (1999). Principals' instructional leadership and teacher development: Teachers' perspectives. *Educational Administration Quarterly, 35*(3), 349-378.

Brookfield, S. (1984). *Adult learning, adult education, and the community.* New York: Teachers College.

Brookfield, S. (1986). *Understanding and facilitating adult learning.* San Francisco, CA: Jossey-Bass.

Clandinin, D. J., & Connelly, F. M. (2000). *Narrative inquiry: Experience and story in qualitative research.* San Francisco, CA: Jossey-Bass.

Edwards, M. (2004). *Civil Society.* Cambridge, UK: Polity Press.

Fosnot, C. (1996). *Constructivism: Theory, perspectives, and practice.* New York: Teachers College.

Knowles, M. (1984). Introduction: The art and science of helping adults learn. In M. Knowles (Ed.), *Andragogy in action: Applying the modern principles of adult learning.* San Francisco, CA: Jossey-Bass.

Mezirow, J. (1990). *Fostering critical reflection in adulthood: A guide to transformative and emancipatory learning.* San Francisco, CA: Jossey-Bass.

Pratt, D. D. (1993). Andragogy after twenty-five years. In S. Merriam (Ed.), *Adult learning theory: An update* (pp. 15-25). San Francisco, CA: Jossey-Bass.

Schön, D. (1983). *The reflective practitioner.* New York: Basic Books.

Schön, D. (1987). *Educating the reflective practitioner.* San Francisco, CA: Jossey-Bass.

Schön, D. (1988). Coaching reflective teaching. In P. Grimmett, P. & G. Erickson (Eds.), *Reflection in teacher education.* New York: Teachers' College.

White, T. H. (1987). *The once and future king.* New York: Ace.

Chapter 6
The Essential Focus
Classroom Practice

Introduction

> More can be done to improve education by improving the effectiveness
> of teachers than by any other factor.
> Wright, Horn, & Sanders, 1997, p. 63

Most critical determinants of a school's effectiveness should be observable in the individual classrooms of the school. In other words, the degree to which a school can be assessed as effective is determined to a great extent by the quality of teaching practice. Harris (2002) contends that "highly effective school improvement projects reflect a form of teacher development that concentrates upon enhancing teaching skills, knowledge, and competency" (p. 99).

Current understandings of teaching effectiveness have their roots in research and literature from the 1970s and 1980s. Authors such as Brophy and Good (1986), Good, Grouws, and Ebmeier (1983), Hunter (1982), Joyce and Showers (1982), Rosenshine (1971), and Stallings (1985) helped shape views of teaching, some of which still tend to favor teacher-centered methods over practices that may better accommodate the needs of twenty-first-century learners.

Marzano (2003) argues there are three "teacher-level factors" (p. 76) in classroom practice that account for most of the variance in student achievement. They are instructional strategies, classroom management, and classroom curriculum design. In a similar vein, Fullan, Hill, and Crevola (2006) champion the "overriding importance of just three factors" (p. 32) in explaining student achievement: motivation to learn and high expectations, time on task and opportunity to learn, and focused teaching.

According to these authors, *focused teaching* is further defined as follows:

1) Knowing in a precise way the strengths and weaknesses of each student at the point of instruction through accurate formative assessment.
2) Knowing the appropriate instructional response and, in particular, when and how to use which instructional strategies and resources.
3) Having the classroom structures, routines, and tools to deliver differentiated instruction and focused teaching on a daily basis. (p. 33)

For many teachers, too much of the literature on teaching effectiveness is frustrating because it is based on so many taken-for-granted assumptions, it is insidiously pejorative, it is written specifically for other audiences, or it is not applicable to their particular circumstances. Unfortunately, the gap between what is being written about teaching effectiveness and what many teachers believe can be fairly accomplished appears to be widening, creating issues and concerns that go to the very core of a society's need for education systems that can help address its fundamental problems. While the debate about teaching quality in North America has continued unabated for several decades, it could be argued that teaching effectiveness in public education has generally improved only slightly above levels observed by Sirotnik in 1983, who summed up teaching in the United States public school system as being characterized by persistence, consistency, and mediocrity.

Teaching Effectiveness

Are there any certain measures of teaching effectiveness? Educational literature is replete with scales, checklists, research, and opinion offering varying degrees of confidence about teaching effectiveness and how it should be assessed. As well, most models of teacher evaluation are too often based on assumptions about effectiveness, the assessment of which is powerfully influenced by factors as diverse as the skills of the evaluator, and the political context in which the evaluation occurs.

The creation of *standards of teaching practice* has been a fairly recent development in public education. The set of Knowledge, Skill, and Attribute (KSA) descriptors that follows has been adapted from a document known as the *Quality Teaching Standard* (Alberta Education, 1997). According to this standard, quality teaching occurs when a teacher engages in ongoing analysis of the context and makes decisions about pedagogy that will most likely result in optimum learning by students. Further, according to the *Quality Teaching Standard*, it is reasonable to expect all teachers to meet the standard throughout their careers, although teaching practices will vary because each teaching situation is different and changing. Accordingly, reasoned judgment must be used to determine whether the Quality Teaching Standard is being met in any given context.

Knowledge, Skills, and Attributes of Effective Teachers

The following descriptors comprise a repertoire of knowledge, skills, and attributes that effective teachers should be able to demonstrate consistently.

Analysis and Application of Contextual Variables

Effective teachers make pedagogical decisions based on the reasoned analysis of contextual characteristics. Examples of the types of variables that may impact optimum student learning include:

- Demographic variables such as age and gender.
- Students' prior learning.
- Cultural and socioeconomic variables.
- Parental and societal considerations.
- Class size and composition.
- Regional, national, and global influences.
- Inter-agency collaboration.
- Subject area.
- Linguistic abilities.

Subject Knowledge

Effective teachers understand the knowledge, concepts, methodologies, and assumptions of the subject disciplines they teach. This includes an understanding of how knowledge in each discipline is created and organized, and appreciation for the fact that subject disciplines are more than bodies of static facts and techniques – they are complex and evolving. Teachers' understanding extends to relevant technologies, the linkages among subject disciplines, and their relevance and importance in everyday life at the personal, local, national, and international levels. Furthermore, teachers understand that students typically bring preconceptions and understandings to a subject. They use strategies and materials that are of assistance in furthering students' learning.

Approaches to Learning

Most teachers recognize there are many approaches to teaching and learning. Effective teachers appreciate individual differences and believe all students can learn, albeit at different rates and in different ways. They recognize different learning styles and accommodate these differences, including the need to respond to diversity by creating multiple paths to learning for individuals and groups of students, specifically those with unique learning needs. Accordingly, teachers understand the reciprocity between teaching and learning. They recognize the fluidity of the learning process. They are constantly monitor the effectiveness and appropriateness of their practices and students' activities and change them as needed.

Various Levels of Planning

Teachers' plans are grounded in their understanding of contextual variables and are a record of their decisions on what teaching and learning strategies to apply. Teachers appreciate the purposes of short-, medium-, and long-term planning, and know how to translate curriculum and desired outcomes into reasoned, meaningful and incrementally progressive learning opportunities for students. Effective teachers monitor the context, their instruction, and students' learning on an ongoing basis and modify their plans accordingly. In addition, teachers strive to establish candid, open, ongoing lines of communication with students, parents, colleagues, and other professionals so that they can incorporate this information into their planning.

Creating a Learning Environment

Effective teachers create and maintain classrooms that are conducive to student success with learning environments wherein students feel physically, psychologically, socially and culturally secure. Teachers work, independently and cooperatively, to make their classrooms and schools stimulating learning environments. They are respectful of students' human dignity, and seek to establish a positive professional relationship with students characterized by mutual respect, trust, and harmony.

Classroom routines are established that enhance and increase students' involvement in meaningful learning activities. Facilities, materials, equipment, and space are organized in ways that provide all students with equitable opportunities to learn.

Translating Content into Learning

There are many approaches to teaching and learning. Effective teachers know a broad range of instructional strategies appropriate to their area of specialization and the subject discipline they teach, and they know which strategies are appropriate to help different students achieve different outcomes. Teachers clearly communicate to students short- and long-range learning expectations and, then, outline how the expectations will be achieved and assessed. They engage students in meaningful activities that motivate and challenge them to achieve those expectations. They integrate current learning with prior learning, providing opportunities for students to relate their learning to the home, community, and broader environment. Teaching strategies will vary with contextual variables, subject content, desired objectives, and the learning needs of individuals and groups of students.

Assessment of Learning

Effective teachers understand the purposes of student assessment. They know how to assess a range of learning objectives by selecting and developing a variety of assessment techniques and instruments. They know how to analyze and use the results for the ultimate benefit of students. In addition, effective teachers gather and use information about students' learning needs and progress to determine and respond to their learning needs. Teachers use a variety of diagnostic methods that include observing students' activities, analyzing students' learning difficulties and strengths, and interpreting the results of assessments and information provided by students, their parents, colleagues, and other professionals. Teachers also help students, parents, and other educators interpret and understand the results of diagnoses and the implications of these assessments for students. They help students develop the ability to diagnose their own learning needs and to assess their progress toward learning goals.

Furthermore, effective teachers use their interpretations of diagnoses and assessments as well as students' work and results to guide their own professional growth. They assist school councils and members of the community to understand the purposes, meanings, outcomes, and implications of assessments.

Appropriately Integrating Technology

Teachers apply a variety of technologies to meet students' learning needs. Teachers use teaching/learning resources such as the chalkboard, texts, computers, and other auditory, print, and visual media. They maintain an awareness of emerging technological resources. They keep abreast of advances in teaching/learning technologies and how they can be incorporated into instruction and learning. As new technologies prove useful and become more widely available, teachers develop their own and their students' proficiencies in using the technologies purposefully, which may include content presentation, delivery and research applications, as well as word processing, information management, and record keeping. Teachers use electronic networks and other telecommunication media to enhance their own knowledge and abilities, and to communicate more effectively with others. Effective teachers recognize the functions of traditional and electronic teaching/learning technologies. They know how to use and how to engage students in using these technologies to present and deliver content, communicate effectively with others, find and secure information, research, word process, manage information, and keep records.

Sustaining Partnerships

Teachers establish and maintain partnerships among schools, with communities, and within their own schools. Effective teachers understand the importance of engaging parents, purposefully and meaningfully, in all aspects of teaching and learning. They know how to develop and implement strategies that create and enhance partnerships among teachers, parents, and students; they appreciate that student learning is enhanced through the use of home and community resources.

Teachers strive to build partnerships with the home that are characterized by the candid sharing of information and ideas to influence how teachers and parents, independently and cooperatively, contribute to students' learning. They seek out and incorporate community resources into their instruction and encourage students to use home and community resources in their learning. Teachers make connections between school, home, and community in order to enhance the relevance and meaning of learning. Home and community resources are utilized to make learning meaningful and relevant so that students can gain an increased understanding of the knowledge, skills, and attitudes needed to participate in and contribute positively to society.

Contributing to the School and Profession

Teachers engage in activities that contribute to the quality of the school as a learning environment. They work with others to develop, coordinate, and implement programs and activities that characterize effective schools. They know the strategies through which they can, independently and collegially, enhance and maintain the quality of their schools to the benefit of students, parents, community, and colleagues; this includes guiding their actions with a personal, overall vision of the purpose of teaching. They are able to communicate their vision, including how it has changed as a result of new knowledge, understanding, and experience.

Effective teachers understand the legislated, moral, and ethical frameworks within which they work. They recognize they are bound by standards of conduct expected of a caring, knowledgeable, and reasonable adult who is entrusted with the custody, care, or education of students. Teachers recognize their actions are bound in moral, ethical, and legal considerations regarding their obligations to students, parents, administrators, school authorities, communities, and society at large. Teachers acknowledge these obligations and act accordingly.

Teaching as Learning

Effective teachers recognize and embody an appreciation for career-long learning. They know how to assess their own teaching and how to work with others responsible for supervising and evaluating teachers. They know how to use the findings of assessments, supervision, and evaluations to select, develop, and implement their own professional development activities. These career-long learners engage in ongoing professional development to enhance their understanding of and ability to analyze the context of teaching, ability to make reasoned judgments and decisions, and pedagogical knowledge and abilities. They recognize their own professional needs and work with others to meet those needs. They share their professional expertise to the benefit of others in their schools, communities, and profession.

In addition, effective teachers guide their actions by their overall visions of the purpose of teaching. They actively refine and redefine their visions in light of the ever-changing context, new knowledge and understandings, and their experiences. While these visions are dynamic and grow in depth and breadth over teachers' careers, the visions maintain at their core a commitment to teaching practices through which students can achieve optimum learning.

The Issue of Competence

Effectiveness in teaching is more likely to result when teachers have a clear understanding of what constitutes teaching *competence*. The following Competency Checklist can be used to assist teachers who are engaged in reflection and self-assessment. In addition, it can be used by supervisors, administrators, and colleagues to provide direction or feedback to teachers.

Table 12: Self-Assessment Competency Checklist

1. Planning and Preparation

Planning and Preparation	Meeting	Exceeding
a) Demonstrates knowledge and skills in the subject matter of all lessons.		
b) Incorporates a variety of appropriate resources and instructional and assessment strategies into lesson plans and unit plans.		
c) Translates curriculum into relevant and appropriate learning objectives for lessons taught.		
d) Takes into account students' prior learning, learning needs, interests, and student variable such as age, gender, socioeconomic status and cultural/linguistic background.		
e) Organizes content into appropriate components and sequences for instruction.		
f) Plans appropriate content and activities sufficient for the time allotted.		
g) Prepares unit plans that include rationale, overview, learning outcomes, teaching/learning activities, and assessment plan.		
h) Integrates information and communications technology into instruction where appropriate.		
i) Prepares long-term plan(s) for the subjects taught, semester plans (elementary) or course outlines (secondary).		
j) Obtains and organizes equipment and materials for instruction.		

2. Instruction

Communication		
a) Uses clear, fluent, and grammatically correct spoken and written language.		
b) Uses vocabulary appropriate to students' age, background, and interests.		
c) Modulates voice for audibility and expression.		
d) Demonstrates cultural sensitivity in communication and instruction.		

Instruction, cont.

	Meeting	Exceeding
Lesson Introduction		
e) Establishes set: reviews prior learning, identifies lesson objective(s) and expectations, uses motivating attention-getters, provides an overview, and relates the lesson to previous learning.		
General Lesson Development		
f) Incorporates strategies for motivating students using relevant and interesting subject matter and activities.		
g) Presents content in appropriately organized sequences for instruction.		
h) Proceeds in appropriate increments to suit the activity and student response.		
i) Demonstrates subject matter competence during instruction.		
j) Organizes and directs learning for individuals, small groups, and whole classes.		
k) Provides clear directions, instructions, and explanations.		
l) Directs efficient transitions between lessons and from one activity to the next.		
m) Uses a variety of instructional strategies to address desired outcomes, subject matter, varied learning styles and individual needs.		
n) Uses a broad range of instructional strategies specific to subject major.		
o) Uses appropriate materials and resources.		
p) Demonstrates flexibility and adaptability.		
Questioning and Discussion		
q) Asks clearly phrased, well-sequenced questions at a variety of cognitive levels.		
r) Provides appropriate wait-time after posing questions.		
s) Seeks clarification and elaboration of student responses where appropriate.		
t) Leads and directs student participation in class discussion effectively and distributes questions appropriately.		
Focus on Student Learning		
u) Circulates in the classroom, intervening when necessary, checking on individual and group understanding of activity/content.		
v) Recognizes and responds to individual differences and group learning needs.		
w) Reinforces student learning: builds on previous learning, reviews, and re-teaches.		
Closure		
x) Achieves closure for lessons, consolidating ideas or concepts through summaries, reviews, discussion, and applications.		
y) Provides additional work when appropriate and explains assignments fully.		

3. Classroom Leadership and Management

	Meeting	Exceeding
Classroom Leadership		
a) Assumes a leadership role in the classroom, taking charge of classroom activities with confidence, poise, composure, and presence.		
b) Creates and maintains an effective learning environment, with high expectations and standards for student learning; attends to student variables such as age, gender, socioeconomic status, and cultural/linguistic background.		
c) Demonstrates initiative, enthusiasm, and a commitment to the students and subject; models appropriate behaviors.		
d) Establishes positive relationships and a classroom climate based on mutual trust and respect.		
Classroom Management		
e) Clearly defines and reinforces classroom procedures and routines.		
f) Clearly communicates and reinforces expectations for appropriate student behavior.		
g) Monitors student behavior and is aware of student behavior at all times.		
h) Responds to inappropriate behavior promptly, firmly, and consistently, using appropriate responses; follows school discipline policies and procedures.		

4. Assessment

	Meeting	Exceeding
Assessment		
a) Assesses student learning using a variety of appropriate assessment techniques and instruments (e.g., observations, conferences, questioning, checking daily work, performance-based and written assessments, quizzes, tests).		
b) Checks frequently for understanding.		
c) Provides timely and effective feedback for and of learning.		
d) Modifies and adapts teaching based on assessment data; employs alternative teaching strategies to re-teach where required.		
e) Analyzes and evaluates measurement data to assess student learning.		
f) Explains to students how learning will be measured.		
g) Develops and maintains accurate records of student achievement (e.g. grade sheets, databases) and communicates results to students, parents, and the school effectively.		

5. Professional Attributes and Responsibilities

	Meeting	Exceeding
Professionalism		
a) Presents a professional appearance and manner.		
b) Fulfills professional obligations (i.e., punctuality, routine administrative duties).		
c) Demonstrates maturity and professional judgment.		
d) Is knowledgeable about professional issues and demonstrates a commitment to the teaching profession.		
e) Establishes appropriate professional relationships with the educational community and wider community.		
Professional Growth		
f) Accurately assesses and documents the effectiveness of lessons, identifying strengths and weaknesses and making appropriate suggestions for improvements.		
g) Uses the results of student assessment and feedback to improve teaching practices and guide professional growth.		
h) Responds appropriately to feedback from others by listening, interpreting, and implementing suggestions.		
i) Develops and communicates a personal vision of teaching.		
j) Develops a professional portfolio/growth plan including goals, evidence of progress toward goals, reflections on growth, and future goals.		
k) Carries out the roles and responsibilities of a teacher according to school and district policies and other relevant legislation.		
l) Applies the knowledge, skills, and attributes for interim certification appropriately.		
Ethical Conduct		
m) Respects the dignity and rights of all persons without prejudice as to race, religious beliefs, colour, gender, sexual orientation, gender identity, physical characteristics, disability, marital status, age, ancestry, place of origin, place of residence, socio-economic background, or linguistic background.		
n) Treats students with dignity and respect and is considerate of their circumstances.		
o) Does not divulge information received in confidence or in the course of professional duties except as required by law or where to do so is in the best interest of the student.		
p) Does not criticize the professional competence or professional reputation of teachers or other student teachers unless the criticism is communicated in confidence to proper officials, after first informing the individual concerned of the criticism.		

Aligning Collaborative Inquiry with Teaching Effectiveness

Background

Hall and Hord (1984) have been influential in adapting elements of change theory to educational practice. Their Concerns-Based Adoption Model highlights the necessity of understanding *stages of concern*, *levels of use*, and *innovation configurations* to ensure the successful implementation of an educational innovation. They identify seven different stages of concern:

> The[y] range from early "self" type concerns, which are more teacher focused, to "task" concerns, which address the logistics and scheduling arrangements with regard to the use of the innovation, and ultimately to "impact" kinds of concerns, which deal more with increasing the effectiveness of the innovation. Research has indicated that at different points in the change process, different Stages of Concern will be more intense. (p. 13)

Glickman (1993) describes a three-phase process teachers follow when they seek to implement a change. In the *orientation* phase, teachers are concerned about the new skills and knowledge they will have to learn and the effects the innovation will have on their current practice. During the *integration* phase, teachers concentrate on exploration, implementation, and feedback. In the *refinement* phase, teachers focus more on exploring, brainstorming, trouble-shooting, and problem solving in their own classrooms, and then extend this to their work with colleagues.

An Alternate Model

When teams of teachers are first asked to identify some aspect of their classroom practice to which they want to devote more attention, a majority raise concerns about student behavior. Their first choices for school-based projects featuring various forms of collaborative inquiry are often replete with references to "kids who can't sit still," or "students who can't follow simple directions," or "students whose character development is seriously deficient."

As teachers move beyond concerns about behavior, they are more willing to focus on curriculum content in particular subject areas. For many teachers, this may be the first time they have studied their curriculum in such detail and, for many of them, it is a liberating and empowering experience. Knowledge of curriculum, gained and shared through collaborative effort, contributes noticeably to teacher confidence, and strongly influences the quality of subsequent conversations about their work. With that confidence, teachers seem more willing to enter into discussions about assessment of student learning. For example, they can be heard to ask each other, "If this is what we have to teach, how will we test it? What are we going to accept as evidence that students have learned it?"

In turn, greater confidence with assessment allows teachers to enter into a more sophisticated examination of student learning. At this stage, there is a greater likelihood that teachers will engage in conversations about such topics as learning styles, brain-based learning, multiple intelligences, constructivism, and the more effective use of Individual Education Plans.

As teams of teachers collaborate to stitch together the tapestry of their practice through trial-and-error, regular sharing of progress, and increasingly meaningful reflection, they display greater curiosity about the ways their colleagues teach, and they express more interest in a wider variety of teaching strategies. Conversations about such topics as differentiated instruction, cooperative learning, inquiry-based teaching, the infusion of technology, and general teaching effectiveness occur with greater regularity. As trust develops, classroom observations are seen to be more helpful than threatening, and are more likely to occur, as are requests for demonstrations by teachers known to be expert in the use of certain practices. In addition, interschool visits are more likely to happen and, slowly, exchanges of visits by teachers in the same school may become more common.

This model of stages of concern is not necessarily linear. Clearly, teachers can engage successfully in using more complicated teaching methods even as they continue to work on matters relating to classroom management, for example. The larger lesson is that teachers who are excessively concerned about student misbehavior are not always able to enter into productive dialogue about such things as metacognition or critical thinking. If their concerns about behavior are at the forefront of their thinking, they will tend to dismiss much of the good that others see in more advanced stages of concern as simply being irrelevant, inapplicable, or even lacking in common sense.

Moreover, even when things are going reasonably well, the closer teams move to being able to observe and share their understanding of the quality of teaching and learning happening in their classrooms, the more likely some team members are to seek to avoid that experience. The following figure describes the progression of concerns for many teachers participating in collaborative inquiry projects.

Figure 13: Progression of Focus and Concerns for Teachers Participating in Collaborative Inquiry

Student Behavior Concerns
How can I provide individual attention to high needs students? How can I differentiate my teaching when students won't sit still?

My Own Teaching
How does constructivist teaching affect my students' engagement levels? What do I do during class time to minimize the gap between high and low achieving students?

Curriculum Content
What are the essential learnings in my content area? How can I ensure my students are ready for standardized tests?

Others' Teaching
How do successful teachers get all students to achieve? Who are some of the teachers who are successfully differentiating their instruction? How do successful teachers deal with criticism from other educators.

Assessment
What is the difference between assessment for and of learning? How can I be sure that using a variety of assessment strategies will positively impact my students' test scores?

Student Learning
How does brain-based teaching influence my students' learning? How do individual learning styles impact my subject area?

Linking the Individual with the Collaborative

When teams of teachers are collaborating effectively, the translation of curriculum outcomes into year plans, unit plans, and daily lesson plans is less of a challenge for them. However, that kind of work is still essentially preliminary. Much of the rhetoric about school improvement and teaching effectiveness is transformed into reality only when teachers are clearly focused on the quality of teaching and learning that is happening in their own classrooms, and openly sharing that knowledge with colleagues. That's when teachers are most likely to get the most accurate assessment of how well their school is doing. Ironically, when school improvement initiatives fall on hard times, one of the first things lost is that willingness of teachers to share their classroom experiences with colleagues and to persist with forms of evidence-based practice that largely depend for their success on collaboration. At those times, principals and other leaders must show their mettle. They must be able to create the time and space for purposeful teacher collaboration and, more importantly, they must be able to encourage, support, and inspire their teachers to continue to do what they know they must do to achieve their goals. At such times, the moral purpose of schools and staffs is most easily identified and understood.

Maintaining Momentum

Teams of teachers are most likely to work together to achieve their goals if they have had opportunities to help create those goals. In turn, they are then more likely to organize their work-lives around their own Professional Growth Plans. Once again, Growth Plans that have been developed by teachers in collaboration with each other, and in harmony with school goals, are those that are most likely to be followed.

The following template can be used by individual members of a collaborative inquiry team to outline and align the contributions they will make to the larger school improvement effort.

When these growth plans are shared among members of collaborative inquiry teams, the chances of goal-achievement are increased. Public commitments to personal plans strengthen the likelihood that all participants will make a genuine contribution to project success.

The following example illustrates an alternate form of growth plan used successfully by a collaborative inquiry team in a school improvement project at the middle school level.

Figure 14: Professional Goals and Growth Plan Template

Professional Goals and Growth Plan Template

Name: _____   School: _____

Principal/Administrator: _____   Year: _____

A. Professional Goals

Goal #1: Rationale (alignment with school goals, strategic plan, student learning, etc.)

_____

_____

Goal #2: Rationale (alignment with school goals, strategic plan, student learning, etc.)

_____

_____

B. Strategies (How will I go about achieving my goals?)

For Goal # 1 (materials, resources, events):

_____

_____

For Goal # 2 (materials, resources, events):

_____

_____

C. Indicators of Progress/Evidence of Completion

For Goal # 1 (student learning indicators):

_____

_____

For Goal # 2 (student learning indicators):

_____

_____

D. Timeline for Completion

	Activity	Due Date
Goals 1		
Goal 2		

E. Summary of Growth and Goals Achieved

_____

_____

F. Reflection on Professional Growth

_____

_____

Figure 15: Teacher's Professional Growth Plan

	Teacher's Professional Growth Plan For: Year: Question of Inquiry: How can I better meet the learning needs of my students?
Personal Goal In line with district & school goals of creating a community of learners.	To incorporate brain-based teaching practices into my classroom, providing an environment of relaxed alertness, immersing students in complex experiences and focusing on active processing.
Timeline Sept-June 2006 Re-evaluate in May/June for 2006.	• Begin to increase # of brain-based strategies and activities at beginning of the year from zero to 1/class. • Continue to increase throughout the semester (2-3 per class). • During creation of resources for 2 new classes from February to June, incorporate strategies directly into lesson plans.
Rationale Improving districts and schools have a thorough and connected set of reasons, based on evidence, for the selection of their student achievement goals.	• Through my research and collaboration with two other teachers, I have been able to explore brain-based teaching and its implications for student learning. I know I need to give my students the best possible environment for learning and I believe brain-based teaching is a way to help me get there. • My responsibility as a teacher is to help students achieve to their highest potential. • I will be teaching with a group of teachers in a pod system next year and I will be able to share my learning with them in a way that we can create interdisciplinary/thematic links between curriculum.
Resources Improving districts and school recognize the experts within their schools as well as experts in the field.	• A variety of articles, texts, and web sites related to brain-based learning and teaching, from a number of experts such as Renate and Geoffrey Caine, John Bruer, Pat Wolfe, Michael Slavkin, Brian Dwyer, Eric Jensen, Sylwester, and others. • The literature synopsis that will be created by myself and two other teachers. • Other experienced peers, administration, AISI teachers, parents, and students. • Curriculum team & Pod team teacher members.
Strategies Improving schools and districts have well-organized, focused improvement plans in place. The strategies selected to achieve the goals are an intelligent blend of research, best practice, and innovative thinking.	• Use knowledge gained this summer to begin incorporation. • Attend Special Education Conference in Edmonton and make brain-based learning sessions a priority. • Observe and confer with colleagues who use or know something about BBL. • Attend workshops offered throughout the year. • Continue to research and read about brain-based learning and teaching in the classroom. • Ask for feedback from students and peers on teaching practices. • Use resources and plan daily activities and schedule time so that brain-based learning techniques become embedded in the curriculum. • Regular pod meetings (once a week) to discuss and collaborate on teaching.
Anticipated	• Class will be enriched with a variety of activities, time will be structured with breaks and more movement.

Building Trust

Collaboration is not automatic. As teachers work together, they certainly develop an appreciation for each other's expertise but they also become more aware of differences in beliefs and attitude that, unexamined, can lead to misunderstanding and unintended conflict.

One area of professional practice about which teachers have deep differences of opinion is that of classroom assessment. Some teachers grade all student work with vague deference to the normal distribution curve. Others grade exclusively on the basis of mastery, while others provide no numerical information in their assessment of student learning, and still others strive to equate student learning with grade level equivalencies. When groups of teachers get together to share units of work and create common assessments, they frequently proceed on the assumption that all of them assess learning in the same ways, and that every collaboratively-developed common assessment will be administered and marked in a uniform way, producing results that are unquestionably comparable across classrooms and schools.

The following activity has the potential to bring to the surface many competing points of view about assessment of learning and student evaluation. In particular, it will bring into sharp focus several issues and concerns that present a powerful challenge to educators' beliefs about assessment and many current assessment practices.

The Spelling Test: Assessment of Student Learning

Under the guidance of a facilitator, this activity is suitable for all sizes of school staffs and all grade levels. It requires a sufficient number of copies of the Test and the Scoring Key as well as template large enough (Whiteboard, Smartboard) to accommodate all the information from every small group.

Figure 16: Spelling Test Activity

Directions For **Individual** Activity

1. Ask participants to mark Jean-Paul's Spelling Test individually, using only their own skills and knowledge. Once they have marked the test they can make note of the number correct out of 50, and record that answer (on the back of the test page) as *STEP A*.
2. Pass out the Test Key. Ask participants to mark the test again, individually, using the Key as a guide. They can record this answer as *STEP B*.
3. Ask participants to convert Jean-Paul's mark, with the Key, into a percentage. They can record this answer as *STEP C*.
4. Ask participants to decide, individually, what letter grade they will give to Jean-Paul's test. They can assign only A, B, C, D, or F. In this school district they do not use (+) or (-). They can record this answer as *STEP D*.

5. Ask participants, individually, to reconsider the letter grade they gave Jean-Paul's test based on the following information about the test results in his homeroom class:

    Highest Score   48
    Lowest Score   23
    Average Score   34

    - Jean-Paul's score is one of the top five.
    - There are 27 students in this homeroom.
    - They can record this answer as *STEP E.*

6. Ask participants, individually, to reconsider their letter grade based on the following information about results for the whole school:

    - There are nine Grade 9 classes in the school.
    - A total of 247 students wrote the Spelling Test.

    Highest Score   50
    Lowest Score   5
    Average Score   25

    - Jean-Paul's score was in the top ten.
    - They can record this answer as *STEP F.*

Directions For **Small Group** Activity

1. Ask participants to form small group of four to six people.
2. Ask them to repeat all the activities they had just done individually by moving through each step and trying to achieve group consensus. They can use whatever strategies they want to complete this section of the activity.
3. Once every group has completed the assigned tasks, begin the process of debriefing.
4. Start by recording information from each group on the following chart:

	GP. 1	GP. 2	GP. 3	GP. 4	GP. 5	GP. 6
Range of Individual Scores Without the Key (STEP A)						
Range of Individual Scores With the Key (STEP B)						
Range of Percentages of Scores With the Key (STEP C)						
Range of Individual Grades for STEP D						
Range of Individual Grades for STEP E						
Range of Individual Grades for STEP F						
Final Grade, Group Consensus						

5. Invite participants to comment on any aspect of the data display that has just been created.
6. Encourage participants to analyze the information, examine the implications of such outcomes, summarize, and draw conclusions.
7. Conclude the activity with an opportunity for participants to share their feelings, and explain what they think they learned from the experience.

The Annual Test of Language Arts Basic Skills (LABS)

Name: _Jean - Paul H._   Class: <u>Grade 9</u>

1. _drying_
2. _chauffeur_
3. _misspelled_
4. _cemetery_
5. _sacreligious_
6. _consceintious_
7. _~~bas~~ liaison_
8. _ninth_
9. _aquisition_
10. _kolleagues_
11. _accomodate_
12. _wholly_
13. _hypocrisy_
14. _quizzes_
15. _reserboir_
16. _pre~~ceed~~cede_
17. _unparalelled_
18. _manageable_
19. _penicillen_
20. _commemorate_
21. _vengeance_
22. _shiek_
23. _~~emm~~igrate_ (em.)
24. _separate_
25. _mischievous_

26. _recommend_
27. _desert_
28. _personnel_
29. _immigrant_
30. _weird_
31. _attendance_
32. _independent_
33. _descendant_ (x a)
34. _pasttime_
35. _peaceable_
36. _connoisseur_
37. _bachelor_
38. _offered_
-39. _fulfillment_
40. _manoeuvre_
41. _vaccuum_
42. _rhythmic_
43. _monetary_
44. _reign_
45. _villain_
46. _reminiscence_
47. _~~ferry~~ fiery_
48. _prominent_
49. _attendance_
50. _~~gage~~ gauge_

The Annual Test of Language Arts Basic Skills (LABS)

Name: <u>Key</u>   Class: <u>Grade 9</u>

1. dyeing
2. chauffeur
3. misspelled
4. cemetery
5. sacrilegious
6. conscientious
7. liaison
8. ninth
9. acquisition
10. colleagues
11. accommodate
12. wholly
13. hypocrisy
14. quizzes
15. reservoir
16. precede
17. unparalleled
18. manageable
19. penicillin
20. commemorate
21. vengeance
22. sheik
23. emigrate
24. separate
25. mischievous

26. recommend
27. dessert
28. personnel
29. immigrant
30. weird
31. attendance
32. independent
33. descendent
34. pastime
35. peaceable
36. connoisseur
37. bachelor
38. offered
39. fulfillment
40. manoeuvre
41. vacuum
42. rhythmic
43. monetary
44. reign
45. villain
46. reminiscence
47. fiery
48. prominent
49. attendance
50. gauge

Classroom Observations and Conferences

As teams of teachers accept increasing responsibility for school improvement, they come face-to-face with a concern that goes deep into the culture of many school communities. The teachers want to see each other teach, and they want to show others those aspects of their own teaching performance in which they have a fair measure of confidence but there are no appropriate structures in place to assist them in their efforts. The existing value system in the school rarely encourages such openness around matters of professional practice. Moreover, most schools still default classroom observations to administrators only, and therein lies the core of the problem.

Most teachers have some unpleasant memories of classroom observations and subsequent conferences that were visited on them for purposes of evaluation. Whether they happened during student teaching, or at other career stages, the negative effects of these *supervision-for-evaluation* events often outweighed the benefits teachers may have derived from the experience. This alone may account for much of the hesitation and skepticism teachers evince when they are invited to participate in cycles of peer consultation designed to promote a deeper understanding of classroom practice. Typically, many teachers will say they don't feel confident enough to share their practice with others. They often give indications that they don't think their teaching is "good enough" for colleagues to see, or they will offer to present "when they've had more time to get it right." Who could blame teachers for their reluctance or avoidance when the negative experiences many teachers encountered in their early years are only compounded by the culture of most schools is still dominated by norms of privatism and segregation?

Teachers have to be convinced of the benefits of such collaboration, not just once but many times over. How can this be done? They need to have all the possibilities for productive classroom observations and conferences explained to them in language that is as free from jargon as possible. They need to see and hear from colleagues who have benefited from the experience. They need strong assurances of safety and, especially, confidentiality. A betrayal of confidentiality in this critical stage of teachers' professional growth can damage the cohesion of school teams even more quickly than gratuitous criticism. They need support and encouragement as they engage in their provisional attempts to master the skills of observing accurately, providing useful feedback, communicating clearly, and maintaining a disciplined approach to the whole process. Above all, they need dedicated time during the school day to do these things as part of their regular work.

How Can Classroom Observations Work?

It bears repeating: teachers are most likely to participate in various forms of peer consultation when they take place in a climate of trust and mutual respect. When these conditions are met, teachers are better able to adapt and modify their teaching practices as they are provided with persuasive evidence of the need for change, particularly if they are given choices about possible directions they can follow.

Some of the most persuasive feedback teachers can receive comes via video. Carefully selected teaching episodes, shared with respectful colleagues, give most teachers the clearest understanding of how well they are performing in the classroom, and which aspects of their practice they would like to change. The conversations with colleagues that accompany the screening of a teaching episode can help teachers refine and confirm their commitment to future action.

Of course, for those teachers who are not ready or willing to watch themselves on video, there are many other tried and proven ways for colleagues to help each other. For example, team teaching is a powerful strategy for developing changes in teaching practice. Having a colleague observe a class and focus on one or more aspects of practice about which a teacher is curious or concerned can produce a lot of useful information that has the potential to be transformed into more effective ways of teaching. Observing colleagues for the specific purpose of learning more about how they teach can result in improvements for all parties. Again, much of the success of these strategies is dependent upon the quality of discussion that accompanies them.

The following case study is an excellent example of the impact of peer supervision, the use of video, and the value of genuine collaboration in helping a school team achieve improvements in teaching practice.

Case Study of the Essential Focus: The Power Within

The staff at Blackstone School had made a lot of progress towards their goal of improving classroom practice. They had conducted study groups on new teaching strategies, tried to introduce new strategies into their classrooms, and discussed these efforts in several team meetings. They had created bulletin boards displaying student work that resulted from their efforts, and they had attended a number of conferences as a school-wide team. They were now ready to move to the next stage, which involved videotaping teaching episodes that they could share and discuss with each other.

In preparation, they used two team meetings to explore the process of observation-and-conference and establish "ground rules" for this activity. Preliminary practice sessions revealed that teachers were not very confident in their ability to engage colleagues in productive conversations about actual teaching practice. They tended to make an excessive number of statements of praise and judgment. They expressed more opinions about each teaching episode than were expressed by the person who did the teaching. They found they were not adept at asking the kinds of questions they wanted to ask, and they were not very helpful in encouraging their colleagues to achieve much depth of reflection about their teaching.

Cycles of practice, feedback, and discussion produced consensus on a set of guidelines that were applied to subsequent sessions. Participants agreed to talk less and listen more; ask questions, the answers to which they did not know, or did not *think* they knew; avoid criticism and use generalized praise in a judicious way; encourage the teacher to offer more analysis and opinion about the teaching episode than they did; and be more aware of the non-verbal cues that each teacher exhibited.

The principal was the first to volunteer. He showed a twenty-minute clip of his Grade 8 students engaged in an inquiry process. Before he started the video he appeared calm and collected, cracking jokes and helping everyone feel at ease. He showed no sign of nervousness or trepidation.

Once the video began, he sat very close to the monitor, almost with his back to the other participants. He let the video run without interruption while the rest of the staff watched attentively until the episode was finished. Immediately, the group produced a collective sigh, almost as if in relief that the hardest part was over. Little did they know!

In accordance with their established procedures, the demonstrating teacher (in this case, the principal) was given the opportunity to speak first. With no hesitation, he launched into an animated commentary about his and his students' enjoyment of the experience, the impact of the camera in the classroom, the learning he saw happening, and his relief that it was over. But, of course, it wasn't over. It hadn't really begun yet!

After some initial questions from the group about the work done by individual students and their use of various media, the principal was asked if he could explain his goals for the lesson. At this point, his pattern of response changed dramatically. Just as he seemed ready to give an instant, not-too-serious answer, he suddenly stopped talking for almost ten seconds before he offered a long, thought-filled explanation, replete with references to many different students and their learning. It was as if he was replaying parts of the lesson over in his mind and seeking out the impor- tance of those highlights in informing his understanding of his own teaching: his insight and understanding seemed to be growing right before the eyes of his staff!

As this powerful drama unfolded, spurred on by questions from the group, the principal provided a wide-ranging presentation of his passion for teaching, his per- sonal philosophy, some career highs and lows, and ended with a heartfelt expression of appreciation for his community and his teaching staff. The principal told every- one that the experience of watching himself teach, and seeing his students doing far better than he thought they were doing during the lesson, really triggered some strong emotions for him. He spoke of feeling at once proud and humble; of being sure that his decision not to leave teaching was so right; of feeling that there were so many more things he wanted to try in subsequent classes; of knowing so much and knowing so little at the same time.

It was a phenomenally emotional event and, before it was over, the principal and several staff members were openly crying. When he concluded, it was very clear to everyone that they had participated in something quite special. As they reflected on their feelings, the teachers spoke of their pride in working with a principal who could lead by example, one who would not expect them to do something he was not prepared to do, too. They spoke of the memories of their own teaching experiences that his comments had rekindled, and all of them indicated their increased willing- ness to share their teaching with their colleagues.

The success of that first round of observation and discussion influenced all sub- sequent sessions as, over the next few months, seven more teachers took their turn. With each new presentation, group confidence grew in harmony with communica- tion skills and mutual trust. A more specific language – more *professional*, perhaps – seeped into the daily staff discourse, as theoretical connections between professional development and classroom teaching were confirmed and refined through experi- ence and practice. As well, all participants came to appreciate the difference between being one of many observers and being in what came to be called the "hot seat". For some, being the focus of so much attention produced something akin to euphoria. One teacher exclaimed, "I have NEVER had a chance to talk about my teaching like that!" Another teacher described how she had developed a completely different appreciation for her colleagues "as human beings" as a result of watching them teach.

This staff continues to work closely together, although two teachers have been promoted to leadership positions in other schools. The work of the staff is character- ized by an ethos of joint responsibility, with teachers willingly engaging in shared leadership. Despite being given an opportunity to transfer to a larger school, the principal has stayed, certain he can continue to make a useful contribution in a school and community where goal-focused work is accomplished in an atmosphere of mutual respect and mutual trust.

Studying the Case Study: You have the power.

- ☑ Identify the critical stages of teacher growth revealed in this scenario.
- ☑ Why might this process be such an emotional one for teachers?
- ☑ What must staff teams do to ensure that norms of confidentiality, trust, and mutual respect are maintained throughout this process?
- ☑ In what ways does this sharing of teaching experiences enhance professional growth?

Understanding the Essential Focus: How To Do It!

The Process
1. Collaborate with all staff in creating a school improvement focus for the year. This may be based on a long-term strategic plan, school goals, or an ad hoc project.
2. Appreciate the power of the authentic curiosity of professional colleagues.
3. Structure team activities in ways that build upon teachers' knowledge of curriculum, assessment, and teaching practice.
4. Make the process inclusive; allow participants to engage when they are ready.
5. Don't strive for perfection as much as for growth and understanding.

The Tools
1. Make sure that school teams have a clear purpose, direction, and time to do the work.
2. Maintain simple but accurate records of team activities.
3. Include as a member of the team at least one administrator, whose responsibilities include making an active contribution to the team's success.
4. Encourage participants to link the work of their teams directly to school goals and professional growth plans.
5. Make sure all the activities have a direct link to student learning.

The Outcomes

1. Don't be reluctant to make evidence of student learning a measure of team success.
2. Provide multiple opportunities for practice and reflection.
3. Provide many opportunities for participants to experience formal and informal leadership opportunities.
4. Honor colleagues' commitment and effort. Celebrate learning!

References

Alberta Education. (1997). *Teaching quality standard applicable to the provision of basic education in Alberta.* Ministerial Order(#016/97). Author.

Brophy, J., & Good, T. (1986). Teacher effects. In M. C. Wittrock (Ed.), *Handbook of research on teaching* (3rd ed.). New York: Macmillan.

Fullan, M., Hill, P., & Crevola, C. (2006). *Breakthrough.* Thousand Oaks, CA: Corwin Press.

Glickman, C. (1992). *Leadership for learning.* Alexandria, VA: ASCD.

Good, T., Grouws, D., & Ebmeier, H. (1983). *Active mathematics teaching.* New York: Longman.

Hall, G., & Hord, S. (1984). *Change in schools: Facilitating the process.* New York: State University of New York Press.

Harris, A. (2002). *School improvement: What's in it for schools?* New York: RoutledgeFalmer.

Hunter, M. (1982). *Mastery teaching.* El Segundo, CA: TIP Publications.

Joyce, B., & Showers, B. (1982). The coaching of teaching. *Educational Leadership, 40*(1), 4-10.

Marzano, R. (2003). *What works in schools: Translating research into action.* Alexandria, VA: ASCD.

Rosenshine, B. (1971). *Teacher behaviors and student achievement.* London: National Foundation for Educational Research.

Sirotnik, K. (1983). What you see is what you get: Consistency, persistence, and mediocrity in classrooms. *Harvard Educational Review, 53*(1), 16-31.

Stallings, J. (1985). A study of implementation of Madeline Hunter's model and its effects on students. *Journal of Educational Research, 78,* 325-337.

Wright, S., Horn, S., & Sanders, W. (1997). Teacher and classroom context effects on student achievement: Implications for teacher evaluation. *Journal of Personnel Evaluation in Education, 11,* 57-67.

Chapter 7
The Essential Commitment
Gathering Evidence of School Improvement

Introduction

School and system evaluations – when they occur – are still conducted by teams comprised primarily of members external to the system, assisted by a lesser number of internal participants. Typically, terms of reference are negotiated in advance, letters of transmission exchanged, contracts formalized, schedules of classroom or office visits developed, and the ordeal begins. Lesson plans and curriculum documents get dusted off, old wardrobes re-appear, suits and briefcases dominate hallways and staff rooms and then, after about ten days, all returns to "normal." Two or three months later, an official report is presented to the school board, even as the evaluation event is passing into memory.

Townsend & Adams, 2005, School System Evaluation

Influential literature on school improvement and change indicates that schools move forward when they are able to align many internal variables such as mission, vision, goals, values, culture, organizational structure, knowledge, and resources with external variables such as policy initiatives, funding, expertise, and expectations. Without doubt, "principals working with teachers are essential to the development of collaborative cultures" (Fullan, 2001, p. 17), and school improvement appears to be dependent, ultimately, on the ability of school staffs to work collaboratively to such a degree that they are able to share and solve, over time, "problems of instructional practice at ever-increasing levels of complexity and demand" (Elmore, 2004, p. 54).

What can be done to get schools started on a path to improvement? Initially, educators must guard against the self-fulfilling power of taken-for-granted assumptions such as "There is only one best way for schools to improve!" or "The best measures of school improvement are external achievement test results." It may be more helpful to be guided by Sergiovanni's (2000) contention that "good schools improve one at a time . . . they improve on their own terms . . . [and] are unique because they reflect the communities they serve" (p. 22).

Clearly, positive change in schools requires persistence, commitment, adequate resources, and effective leadership. Whether the improvement efforts are organized at a system or site level, school staffs are most likely to make productive links between professional development and improved student learning when their professional growth activities are job-embedded and relate to the immediacy of their teaching practice. In addition, some form of purposeful collaboration appears essential if school staffs are to achieve their agreed-upon goals, the most critical of which should focus on student learning. Finally, the careful documentation of school improvement efforts through a clearly identified inquiry process increases the likelihood of success and continuity. Once individual school staffs have achieved a certain level of success, they are better able to share their experiences with colleagues in other schools. More importantly, they are more likely to understand and appreciate the accomplishments of colleagues in other schools.

Sustainability

When teachers and principals try to do everything, everything gets done less well. When school-based teams take on too much work in addition to their regular duties, they rarely seem to have enough time to accomplish tasks to their own satisfaction. They come to resent time away from their schools and classrooms. Time for collaboration becomes compressed. Time for deeper thinking gets curtailed.

The design of models of school improvement and professional growth must include safeguards against a tendency to equate sustainability with the implication that regardless of how much improvement teachers accomplish, they will never be good enough. Images of teacher growth and professional development as a constant upward incline do not adequately attend to basic precepts of adult learning. Adult learning is a cyclical process in which time for reflection, adaptation, and refinement of practice is at least as important as the evidence of momentum. Moreover, when school teams experience success, they are more likely to see links between their learning and the learning of students. The cyclicity of the process is compelling: the more knowledgeable and skilful teachers become, the more they understand how and why students learn better, and the more students will learn.

A common factor in all of this is that of *time*. In schools, excessive amounts of effort and energy are expended on projects and initiatives that are done in a hurry. It seems there is always time to do things over and over again in a rush, but rarely do school teams take time to do the work of improvement as well as it can be done *the first time, carefully and thoughtfully*. Profiles of school improvement activities show an entrenched tendency for schools to move from one big, new idea to another, virtually on a yearly basis. Leaders of school improvement initiatives must take greater responsibility for ensuring that every initiative is accorded the amount of quality time that is fundamental to its successful implementation.

Another imperative of school improvement is that participants must learn to do *enough*. Sustainability of school improvement is analogous to the sustainability of quality relationships – it takes commitment, persistence, and a measure of luck. The idea of sustainability is not merely to create conditions under which schools are more able to do the same things over and over again. Rather, it should create in schools the capacity to continuously do the *right* things. In reality, this definition speaks to quality versus quantity. Successful school teams engage in cycles of learning rather than in episodes of learning and, in reality, their learning through collaborative inquiry complements their career development as educational practitioners.

Sustainability is not just another item to be crossed off a checklist. Sustainability is a characteristic of those school improvement initiatives that focus on student learning and continuous professional growth. Schools do not have to ensure that they have conditions of sustainability before they can make progress in school improvement. Rather, schools become more likely to adopt practices and create structures that are sustainable because they adapt and adjust their existing cultures based on persuasive evidence of the positive results of the goal-focused work in which they are engaged.

In summary, when school improvement initiatives are sustained, they have a positive impact on school culture, and they act as an engine for capacity-building. They empower staff, contribute measurably to the development of a heightened sense of community, and generally enhance feelings of efficacy.

Improvement versus Progress versus Change: A Semantic Puzzle

In school improvement, choice of language has the power to influence patterns of commitment and participation. For some school staffs, any talk of the need for *improvement* carries with it undertones of criticism that can trigger negative reactions. Similarly, proposals for *change*, carelessly worded, can help unleash forces of resistance that have the power to severely limit a proposal's chance for success. In some instances, it may be more productive to think of innovative projects as contributing to a sense of continuous *progress* in the life of a school and its educators. Progress can mean change in a positive direction. It can also mean forms of improvement on a great variety of measures more collectively indicative of professional growth than, say, achievement test data. According to this interpretation of progress, schools may be able to provide evidence of goal achievement through a very broad range of measures such as increased professional dialogue, enhanced professional learning, student moral development, student leadership, parent involvement and satisfaction, or changes in classroom practice that hold the potential to lead to further progress every future year.

Most educators accept the assumption that "we can all improve," but they are aware that much change that occurs in school improvement initiatives will not always be in the direction of agreed-upon goals. Some change can be positive, while some can contribute to dysfunction, and some to a loss of learning opportunities. Similarly, the value of the term *improvement* can be compromised when an understanding of its meaning is linked only to the narrowest measures of student achievement. When the terms improvement, change, and progress are synonymous in the minds of participants – and they all carry positive connotations – continued success is more likely.

Something similar happens when school-based teams confront the question, "How will you know that you have been successful?" Too many models of school improvement seem fixated on words such as data, or results, or evidence. Many teachers find the word *data* too clinical for their comfort and, for some, the notion of a *data-driven* school denies the essential human relations that make up school life. Overuse of the term *results* can produce a collective cringe among educators who have learned to interpret a coded meaning of results as referring only to standardized test scores. The word *evidence*, too, has its own baggage, yet school team members seem to warm more quickly to the idea of evidence-based practice than to either data or results. Whatever words are used in identifying goals, or explaining success, they must be as free from negative connotation as possible. They must be *owned* and honored by the men and women who are doing the work on the front line of school improvement – in the classrooms and offices of each improving school.

The success of school improvement initiatives depends so much on the strength of commitment of the classroom teachers who are their most numerous and most influential participants. An old rule of thumb is that in any school improvement work misunderstanding is the *normal* state of affairs. All participants must be aware of the potential for misunderstandings to occur, and take all necessary steps to prevent them from happening. In addition, school improvement initiatives must be planned with due care and attention to strategies for dealing with miscommunications and misunderstandings whenever they arise.

The Politicization of Improvement and Professional Development

Few schools progress at rates that could be described as dramatic, and progress in successful schools is frequently slower, or more incremental, than in schools whose students face greater barriers to learning. Ironically, schools that provide evidence of too much success, or progress too rapidly or noticeably, often generate negative reactions from other schools.

The politics of schools and districts demands that educators be very careful in using the practices of particular schools or their achievements as positive examples, lest they create a climate of comparison – and potential competition – in which some schools and their staffs come to feel they are being unfavorably rated while others appear to be receiving a disproportionate amount of affirmation. One of the great unanticipated results of many school-based projects is the extent to which success in one part of the project has the potential to create negative effects on progress in other parts of the project. All professional development and school improvement activities have the potential to expose sources of conflict, feelings of inadequacy, unresolved issues, and personal histories that can get in the way of project success.

Assessing the Essential Commitment

To the extent that educational initiatives are most commonly evaluated in order to determine past effectiveness and to create future goals, "evaluation is an essential, integral component of all innovative programs" (Somekh, 2001, p. 76). It is "the process of making judgment about the merit, value, or worth of educational programs, projects, materials, and techniques" (Borg & Gall, 1983, p. 733).

It is important that program evaluation not be confused with other forms of inquiry or data collections which are conducted for different purposes (Gredler, 1996). For example, the use of evaluation as a strategy for *program improvement* rather than for accountability, justification, and program continuity has traditionally differentiated *formative* from *summative* evaluation. The latter consists of activities "to obtain some kind of terminal or over-all evaluation in order that some type of general conclusion can be made" (Tyler, Gagne, & Scriven, 1967, p. 86), while formative evaluation takes place at a more intermediate stage, "permit[ting] intelligent changes to be made" (p. 86) as the initiative evolves.

Hopkins (1989) suggests that evaluation in schools should be used for three types of decisions: course improvement (instructional methods and materials); decisions about individuals (pupil and teacher needs); and administrative regulation (rating schools, systems, and teachers). Evaluation *of* school improvement, evaluation *for* school improvement, and evaluation *as* school improvement characterize these three approaches.

An obvious but often overlooked characteristic of the evaluation process is the degree to which results are relevant, functional, and useful. Clearly, an evaluation should not be undertaken if no use is to be made of the results. However, provided the results are produced in a format that is timely, tailored to suit the audience, and reported using appropriate media, educators can use them to plan program improvements. This can lead to a cyclical process in which, "changes in a program may be necessary, benchmarks and results-based goals may need to be redefined, or action strategies may need to be continued, replaced, or redesigned" (Hertling, 2000, p. 3).

Assessing the Essential Commitment: An Alternate Perspective

More recently, another approach to evaluation has slowly gained favor with educators. It has been developed, in part, in response to a concern that increased "politicization of evaluation . . . tight time lines, restricted budgets, and an overemphasis on cost-effectiveness . . . often distort currently accepted evaluation procedures" (Hopkins, 1989, p. 9). For Hopkins, evaluation should be viewed as an illuminative rather than recommendatory exercise, as a guide for improvement rather than evidence for judgment. He promotes the concept of *empowerment* evaluation as a process of program improvement in which participants are helped to conduct their own evaluation.

Empowerment evaluation is a collaborative activity that employs both qualitative and quantitative methods. Teams of educators, with the assistance of trained evaluators, learn to assess, progress towards goals, and reshape the goals according to theoretical foundations. This results in a type of self-determination that Earl (2000) refers to as "agency" (p. 60). Fetterman (2001) suggests that empowerment evaluation fosters self-determination, competence, and independence. It involves a fundamentally democratic process that promotes, among other things, self-awareness, and capacity building. Improvements in the quality of education occur, "not through legislative fiat, but through the exercise and development of professional judgment of those within the system" (Hopkins, 1989, p. 194). A central premise of this method is that efficacy of schools is not contingent on external forces, but on their properties as social systems.

Empowerment evaluation methods question the overly-judgmental nature of traditional evaluation, and seek to moderate the importance of external critique by internalizing self-evaluation processes and practices. Strongly influenced by action research, they are dynamic and responsive approaches that emphasize inclusion rather than exclusion and, unlike other professional development initiatives, they are robust enough to enhance long-term cultural transformation.

Additionally, empowerment evaluation acknowledges the constructivist belief that people can discover knowledge and solutions based on their own experiences. While findings remain grounded in collected data, program stakeholders are able to establish their own goals, processes, outcomes, and impacts. External evaluators are able to provide training, coaching, and assistance in an atmosphere of honesty, trust, support, criticism, and self-criticism. Neither a servant, nor a judge, nor a slave, the external evaluator, seen as a "critical friend" (Earl, 2000, p. 59), can help keep the effort credible, useful, directed, and rigorous, contributing positively to the formation of "a dynamic community of transformative learning" (Fetterman, 2001, p. 6). For empowerment evaluation to be effective and credible, participants must enjoy the latitude to take risks and, simultaneously, assume responsibility. A safe atmosphere, in which it is possible to share success and failure, is as essential as a sense of caring and community.

Posavac and Carey (1997) have adopted a model of program evaluation that honors many of the principles of empowerment evaluation. They contend that their *improvement-focused model* best meets the criteria necessary for effective evaluation. That is, the needs of stakeholders are served; valid information is provided; and alternate viewpoints are acknowledged. As Posavac and Carey note, "to carry this off without threatening the staff is the greatest challenge of program evaluation" (p. 27).

Confirming the Essential Commitment: Generative Evaluation

Evidence-based practice is synonymous with the precepts of collaborative inquiry that, in turn, is highly compatible with methods of program evaluation that honor the expertise and the sensibilities of the people who do the work.

Generative evaluation (Adams & Townsend, 2006) is defined as a method of empowerment evaluation distinguished by its emphasis on:

- Multiple ways of knowing.
- The learning of all participants.
- The value placed on relationships, mutual respect, and trust.
- The purposeful linking of the process to established mission statements, principles, goals, and values.
- The transparency and accessibility of the process.
- The timely and ethical use of new knowledge created through the process.
- the pace of implementation.
- Internal ownership of both the process and the results.

The generative evaluation process attends to relationships and evidence with equal rigor, and it has produced some hopeful results. Its success is clearly dependent on many contextual factors such as the willingness of leaders to take risks and share their authority, extant levels of trust, the adequacy of expertise, and the availability of resources. Effective implementation of a generative model may be equally dependent upon the type and focus of the question that guides the investigation, the sincerity of participants, the quality of pre-existing and evolving relationships, and the levels of support for innovation and improvement in the larger educational system.

As a comprehensive model of evaluation, the generative approach complements the principles of learning communities. It has the potential to create and sustain organizational learning while providing increased opportunities for collaboration, recognition, and celebration. It is a model that demands joint responsibility, built as it is on disciplined inquiry, trust, commitment, and mutual respect.

However, while it is a financially responsible model, the generative approach requires much more time. As well, despite the involvement of large numbers of internal team members, it can nevertheless be the cause of conflict if it appears that participants have been unfairly selected or the focus of the evaluation is obviously biased. It can promote conflict in other ways, too, particularly if it challenges existing power and authority relationships. It could fail if, in its early stages, data reveal concerns or shortcomings with which the educational leaders are not ready or willing to contend. Another risk is that the generative approach could become a self-congratulatory exercise should the integrity of its commitment to ethical uses of all evidence be compromised. Similarly, if the relationship between external and internal team members were to suffer from over-identification (Glesne, 1999), the quality of the evaluation could be eroded.

Why Try Generative Evaluation?

- To change a practice.
- To address a concern.
- To resolve an issue.
- To refine a decision.
- To implement an innovation.
- To answer a question.
- To manage a conflict.
- To provide evidence of change.
- To create more reasons to celebrate.
- To document organizational learning.

The Process: One Example

Step #1: Creating the Team

A generative evaluation initiative typically includes a large numbers of participants and a variety of data collection strategies to provide answers to an inquiry developed through consensus. Depending on the scope and the focus of the evaluation, team members can be drawn from any number of stakeholder groups. Team membership can be invitational and nominational, the primary criterion being that the team comprise enough people, representative of all the groups that will be impacted by the evaluation results.

Step #2: Asking the Question

Once the team is assembled, the first priority is to create a comprehensive question that will guide the evaluation. The *right* question is critical to the success of the evaluation. It will come into clearer focus as team members clarify the outcomes they hope the evaluation will achieve. The *best* question will result from the most open sharing of individual agendas and concerns, from an extended, generative dialogue characterized by collaborative problem-solving. The following question guided the work of the evaluation team in the Bison Lake School District that is the subject of the case study at the end of this chapter.

> What are the resources, processes, structures, strategies, principles, and values that impact school improvement in this district?

Step #3: Strategic Planning

With the question at the centre, and evaluation outcomes clearly stated, the team can then decide on such matters as data collection techniques, timelines, methods of data analysis, a schedule of training opportunities, meeting schedules, and products of the evaluation. The following diagram shows how the evaluation team in Bison Lake School District moved from the question to the subsequent action stages.

Figure 17: Strategic Planning Action Stages

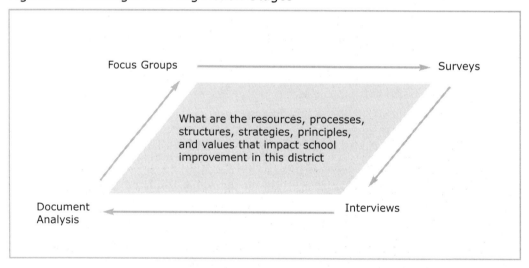

Step #4: Data Collection, Data Analysis, and Training

Each stage of data collection and data analysis should be accompanied by appropriate training provided by either external or internal members of the evaluation team. Team meetings should be planned to coincide with the completion of each stage of data collection, and each meeting should be organized around the three questions that comprise the agenda for collaborative inquiry team meetings:

1. What have we done?
2. What have we learned from that?
3. What will we do next?

A) Focus Groups

The evaluation team selected *focus group meetings* as their first data collection strategy. Team members participated in several training sessions before they were assigned partners and began the process of gathering data from thirty-seven different focus groups throughout the district. The team compiled the following Facilitator's Guide to help them accomplish this task.

Figure 18: Focus Group Facilitator's Guide

Focus Group Facilitator's Guide

Send in advance:

- ☐ Memo to focus group participants
- ☐ Consent forms
- ☐ Description of the collaborative inquiry project

Format of focus group meeting:

- ☐ Partner discussion of question first
- ☐ Partners join with another pair and discuss commonalities of responses
- ☐ Large group reporting; facilitator records comments

Opener:

"Today we are trying to collect information on how work gets done in our school/district."
We hope to talk about examples of the following:

1. Collaboration: How do we work collaboratively together?
2. Leadership: What kinds of things can you say about leadership in this school/district?
3. Shared Vision: What kinds of things can you say about the shared vision of this school/district?
4. Results Orientation: How do you use information (data) in your job?
5. Professional Development: What kinds of things can you say about professional development in this school/district?
6. Continuous Improvement: What kinds of things can you say about continuous improvement in school/district?

Closure: If you could identify one thing that hasn't been addressed here, what would it be?

Follow Up:

- ☐ Summarize the key points the group made
- ☐ Send back to participants in a thank you letter format
- ☐ Confirm or clarify the content of the data collected.

B) Surveys

The analysis of data from any one source should lead an evaluation team to decisions about data sufficiency. Has enough data been collected? Does the team need more data from a different source? Of a different type?

In Bison Lake (the Case Study of the chapter), the team had decided in advance that the focus group data should provide a starting point for the development of a survey. A subgroup of the team put together a first draft of what would eventually become the Learning Communities Questionnaire that appears in Chapter 2 of this text. Surveys were administered to all members of the following stakeholder groups:

- Custodians
- Educational Assistants
- Bus Drivers
- Administrative Support Members
- Facilities and Maintenance Support Members
- Teachers
- School Administrators
- Division Administrators
- Trustees

C) Document Analysis

Glesne (1999) identifies document analysis as one of the three dominant data gathering techniques in qualitative inquiry. The Bison Lake team had decided in their early meetings that some form of document analysis would form part of the data collection strategy. Team members brainstormed a list of school-site and system documents that would illustrate the extent to which the vocabulary and language used therein conformed to the district's stated mission and vision, principles, values, and goals. Accordingly, while the 914 surveys were being completed and collected, team members began the content analysis of hundreds of school and district documents, using the following Document Analysis Template they had developed.

The team used a method of stratified sampling (Neuman, 1997) to determine the schools from which documents would be gathered. Statistical Package for the Social Sciences (SPSS 11.5) was used to analyze the content of documents according to the five themes discussed in detail in Chapter 2: mission and vision, leadership, learning, culture, and organizational structure.

Figure 19: Document Analysis Template

Document Analysis Template

Name of Document: _____
Author: _____
Housing Location: _____
Size: _____
Audience: _____
Uses: _____
Historical Information: _____

Text Analysis:

⮞ **Mission & Vision:** The document aligns with organizational mission, vision, principles, values, and goals.
Comments: _____

Extent to which this characteristic is evident in the document: 0 1 2 3 4 5

⮞ **Leadership:** The document supports the practice of responsible leadership.
Comments: _____

Extent to which this characteristic is evident in the document: 0 1 2 3 4 5

⮞ **Learning:** The document places the learning of children and adults as a central focus.
Comments: _____

Extent to which this characteristic is evident in the document: 0 1 2 3 4 5

⮞ **Culture:** The document supports a culture of trust, collaboration, teamwork, and recognition.
Comments: _____

Extent to which this characteristic is evident in the document: 0 1 2 3 4 5

⮞ **Organizational Structure:** The document supports empowering decision-making structures.
Comments: _____

Extent to which this characteristic is evident in the document: 0 1 2 3 4 5

What, if any, interview questions does this document generate?

1. _____
2. _____
3. _____

D) Interviews

According to Fitzpatrick, Sanders, and Worthen (2004), qualitative interviews are often a key to data collection. They are useful "for learning the perspectives, attitudes, behaviors, and experiences of others" (p. 348). However, as Stake (1975) cautions, "getting acquiescence to interviews is perhaps the easiest task in case study research. Getting a good interview is not so easy" (p. 64).

The Bison Lake team had planned to conduct some interviews but they did not determine how large the interview sample would be until they had analyzed most of the focus group, survey, and document data. Then, they devised the following Sample Interview Questions and Interview Data Analysis Template to assist them in completing this phase.

Figure 20: Sample Interview Questions

Sample Interview Questions

Mission & Vision
- What can you tell me about the mission and vision statements of this school/district?
- What was your level of involvement in the development of this school's/district's mission and vision statements?

Leadership
- What are some of the words you would use to describe the leadership in this school/district?
- Provide an example/story that best represents your understanding or beliefs about leadership.

Culture
- Describe some of the most essential elements of the culture of this school division.
- What is a metaphor that best describes the culture of this school division?

Learning
- Describe some of the ways this school division places primary importance on learning.

For Students	For Staff	For the System

Organizational Structure
- In what ways are our stakeholders encouraged to participate in the decision-making process?
- Suggest ways in which participation can be enhanced.
- In what ways does evaluation contribute to the effectiveness of this school?

For Students	For Staff	For the System

Interviewer Comments: _____

_____

Figure 21: Interview Data Analysis Template

Interview Data Analysis Template

Mission & Vision
- MV 1a. What can you tell me about the mission and vision statements of Bison Lake School Division?

	Knew it	Did not know it	Partially knew it	Generally + statements	Generally – statements
Principals					
Teachers					
CO Staff					
Support					
Students					
Other					
Totals					

- MV 1b. Examples:
- Highlight 2 examples of representative positive statements (YELLOW).
- Highlight 2 examples of representative negative comments (BLUE).
- MV 2a. What was your level of involvement in the development of our mission and vision statements?

	None	Minimal	Moderate	Extensive
Principals				
Teachers				
Co-Staff				
Support				
Students				
Other				
Totals				

- MV 2b. Highlight up to 2 representative statements from each category (NONE-orange
- MINIMAL-purple
- MODERATE-green
- EXTENSIVE-pink)

Interviewer Comments: *Circle in Red* any post-interview comment made by you or a respondent that has not yet been included in the analysis.

_____
_____
_____
_____

Step #5: Verification, Recommendations, and Publication

When the processes of analysis and triangulation of data convince the evaluation team that they can provide a comprehensive answer to their guiding question (and in accordance with established guidelines and timelines), it is time for the publication stage to begin. The team should prepare drafts of each section of evaluation results. These preliminary reports should be shared with all those who contributed to their development so that any errors or omissions can be addressed. Once this process of verification is complete, a final report should be prepared and, first, presented to the School Board or other agency that authorized the evaluation. Once it is accepted at that level, it should be given broad distribution so that a transparency of practice characterizes the process from start to finish.

Step #6: Implement Recommendations and Review the Process

An evaluation should never be undertaken if its results and recommendations are not going to be put to use within a reasonable time frame. In just as timely a fashion, the evaluation process should be reviewed in all appropriate ways so that its most positive features can be more thoughtfully incorporated into subsequent evaluations, and its shortcomings can be addressed.

Step #7: Asking New Questions and Beginning Again

Generative evaluation is analogous to collaborative inquiry, and it is harmonious with the fundamental precepts of learning communities. If schools are moving forward in their improvement goals, generative evaluation is the process of assessment most likely to provide the essential answers about what those schools are accomplishing, while doing the least amount of damage to staff morale and commitment. Put more positively, generative evaluation encourages teachers to take greater control of their professional lives while offering boundless opportunities for the development of skills and knowledge that are essential to career-long professional growth.

Case Study: Bison Lake Generates School Improvement

While neighboring school districts were searching for school improvement solutions in class size formulae, cognitive coaching, and leveled literacy programs, Bison Lake School District – a large rural district of approximately 11 000 students and 600 teachers – was offering incentives of $500.00 to any school that would undertake a school-based project using action research. Five elementary schools and six months later, the Assistant Superintendent in charge of this initiative was pleasantly surprised that such a simple strategy produced such a positive response. In this district, where relations between school staff and central office had sometimes been strained, instances of collaboration were most welcome. This small foray into school-based projects produced a number of unanticipated and unintended outcomes that encouraged the Assistant Superintendent to conduct a more thorough investigation of the potential of this form of school improvement.

In the following year, ten schools signed on to a research-and-development project in which they agreed to try a much more rigorous form of inquiry. They met first as a large group to create and define research questions appropriate to the needs of each school. After that, they met monthly with the Assistant Superintendent and a university researcher to analyze results, document progress, and plan evolving strategies. At the end of the year, every team produced a brief monograph describing their work, its results, and the strengths and weaknesses of the process.

When government funding for innovative school projects became available the following year, this school district was in a strong position to take full advantage of the opportunity. Teams from eighteen schools created inquiry questions that guided the work of their projects for three years. Each project was constructed around goals, targets, measures, and results. Each project was designed to achieve specific student learning outcomes through teacher professional growth. As well, in conjunction with the innovative school projects, the district embarked on an ambitious schedule of professional development for teachers, beginning with literacy and assessment of learning. The combined impact of these two initiatives raised the profile of professional development to levels never before achieved in this district.

It seemed that everyone was involved in some form of professional development and that this was contributing positively to the achievement of district goals. Teachers were clearly happier; principals were more confident; everyone seemed to be working harder, yet contentedly. What could be wrong with that? The Superintendent and Assistant Superintendent were very pleased that their enthusiasm had been so effectively communicated to so many educators. Still, when asked by the School Trustees if all this effort was providing better learning for students, they were forced to pause and reconsider. Their initial response was, "Of course it is!" but, upon further reflection, they had to admit that they were not at all certain. The question was partially answered when the results of a national survey revealed that test scores in this district had been rising steadily for four years. However, that was not enough evidence for these two leaders, in part because those results – while showing improvement – still made evident areas of weakness and deficiency in student learning. Their curiosity to know how extensively their improvement initiatives were impacting schools led these two district office administrators to plan a more thorough assessment of the work of their schools.

They began with a Math program review, the results of which confirmed broad-based progress in critical areas of problem solving and skill development. The Math program review was conducted by a team of thirty educators from within the district and six from without. Buoyed by the results, and spurred on by the desire to know more, leaders in this district – including principals, central office staff, and board members – decided it was time for a review of district operations and a cost analysis of the expansive professional development program.

Each iteration of program evaluation and each new phase of collaborative inquiry enhanced the capacity of district educators to take increasing responsibility for their professional lives. In addition, each evaluation saw refinements being made to the process that were particular to the contexts and personnel of the district. Educators in this district were actively involved in creating new knowledge about learning communities and formulating new strategies for program evaluation, even though they were not fully aware that they were doing so. Critical elements of the Learning Communities Questionnaire that appear in Chapter 2 and the Generative Evaluation model described in Chapter 7 were developed at this time in this district.

The culminating program evaluation extended over parts of three school years. It involved twenty-six representatives of various district stakeholder groups (including students!), and two external researchers. Results provided abundant evidence of a school district moving forward impressively in the achievement of its goals and the professional development of all staff. A comprehensive report of this large program evaluation was broadly disseminated throughout the district. In due course, all the recommendations of the evaluation were given appropriate attention; the implementation of some recommendations began immediately, and the process continued, with purpose, over the ensuing year.

What really happened in this school district over the five-year period? A sustained commitment to improvement and the careful assessment of its impact helped transform this school district from average to excellent in just five years. The district became a leader in the development of educational resources and the preparation of leaders who were enthusiastically recruited by other school districts. It led the way in areas as important as new curriculum implementation, project leadership, and the assessment of student learning. It established itself as a center for the exploration of new ideas, issues, and concerns on subjects as diverse as student achievement, school leadership, and educational decision making.

Most of all, it moved to the forefront in capacity building and succession planning, areas of educational development that plague many districts. It established new standards for school-community relations and employer-employee relations that others districts attempted to emulate. In the final analysis, it succeeded in fully integrating the process of inquiry into "the way work gets done in this district." As the Assistant Superintendent said, "It is ALL collaborative inquiry now . . . It's the way I do my job."

Studying the Case Study: How does *your* district do "improvement"?

- ☑ Describe and analyze a recent school improvement initiative in which you have been involved. In what ways is it similar and different to the Bison Lake School District experience?
- ☑ What aspects of the Bison Lake approach cause you the greatest concern? What aspects would you try to incorporate into your school improvement efforts?
- ☑ What are some of the necessary preconditions that allow or encourage school districts to undertake school improvement initiatives on a scale broad enough to bring about meaningful change?

Evaluating Generative Evaluation: How To Do It!

1. Strive for improvement and embrace change. Change and growth are healthy and necessary components of professional practice.
2. Celebrate professional growth and self-reflection.
3. Welcome the opportunity to participate in collegial and collaborative processes. Much can be accomplished with teamwork. More heads are always better than one!
4. Realize that student contributions are important to the evaluative process. Value student input and insights regarding program success and effectiveness.
5. Agree on key tasks for the evaluation. Work as a team to determine what components are relevant and necessary to evaluate the program or project. The team must agree on important aspects such as data gathering methods, findings, conclusions, and recommendations.
6. Become familiar with research methods and terminology to ensure comfortable participation in the evaluation process.
7. Use a variety of approaches or methods in evaluation. Accurate, balanced evaluations result when multiple strategies are employed.

8. Use evaluation for change and improvement.
9. Keep positive if some things you try don't seem to work at first. That can be a good opportunity to share your experiences with others so that learning can be increased.

References

Adams, P., & Townsend, D. (2006). School and system evaluation: A generative approach. *IEJLL, 10*(6).

Borg, W. R., & Gall, M. D. (1983). *Educational research: An introduction* (4th ed.). New York: Longman.

Elmore, R. (2000). *Building a new structure for school leadership.* Boston, MA: Shanker Institute.

Fetterman, D. (2001). Empowerment evaluation. *Evaluation Practice, 15,* 1-15.

Fitzpatrick, J. L., Sanders, J. R., & Worthen, B. R. (2004). *Program evaluation: Alternative approaches and practical guidelines* (3rd ed.). Boston, MA: Pearson/Allyn and Bacon.

Fullan. M. (2001). *Leading in a culture of change.* San Francisco, CA: Jossey-Bass.

Glesne, C. (1999). *Becoming qualitative researchers: An introduction.* New York: Longman.

Hopkins, D. (1989). *Evaluation for school improvement.* Buckingham, UK: Open.

Neuman, W. L. (1997). *Social research methods: Qualitative and quantitative approaches* (3rd ed.). Boston, MA: Allyn and Bacon.

Posavac, E., & Carey, R. (1997). *Program evaluation: Methods and case studies.* Upper Saddle River, NJ: Prentice-Hall.

Sergiovanni, T. J. (2000). *The lifeworld of leadership: Creating culture, community, and personal meaning in our schools.* San Francisco, CA: Jossey-Bass.

Somekh, B. (2001). The great courseware gamble: The trials and tribulations of a government-funded courseware development project. In D. Murphy, R. Walker, and G. Webb (Eds.) *Online learning and teaching with technology: Case studies, experience and practice* (pp. 121-128). London: Kogan Page.

Stake, R. (1975). *Evaluating the arts in education: A responsive approach.* Columbus, OH: Merrill.

Tyler, R. W. (1967). *Perspectives of curriculum evaluation.* Chicago: Rand McNally.